D0153327

Southern Literary Studies
Louis D. Rubin, Jr., Editor

EXILES AND FUGITIVES

mo.

EXILES AND FUGITIVES

The Letters of Jacques and Raïssa Maritain,
Allen Tate, and Caroline Gordon

edited by
JOHN M. DUNAWAY

Université d'Ottawa
BIBLIOTHÈQUES

LIBRARIES
University of Ottawa

Louisiana State University Press / Baton Rouge and London

Copyright © 1992 by Louisiana State University Press

All rights reserved

Manufactured in the United States of America

First printing

01 00 99 98 97 96 95 94 93 92   5 4 3 2 1

Designer: Amanda McDonald Key
Typeface: Sabon
Typesetter: G & S Typesetters, Inc.
Printer and binder: Thomson–Shore Inc.

The editor is grateful to Helen H. Tate, Nancy Tate Wood, Soeur Marie Pascale, Cornelia Borgerhoff, the Cercle d'Etudes Jacques et Raïssa Maritain in Kolbsheim, Alsace, and Princeton University Library for permission to reprint these letters.

The Introduction first appeared, in somewhat different form, as "Exiles & Fugitives: The Maritain-Tate-Gordon Letters," in *From Twilight to Dawn: The Cultural Vision of Jacques Maritain*, ed. Peter A. Redpath (Notre Dame, 1990), and is reprinted by permission.

Library of Congress Cataloging-in-Publication Data

Exiles and fugitives : the letters of Jacques and Raïssa Maritain,
    Allen Tate, and Caroline Gordon / edited by John M. Dunaway.
        p.   cm. — (Southern literary studies)
    Includes index.
    ISBN 0-8071-1779-X (alk. paper)
    1. Maritain, Jacques, 1882–1973—Correspondence.
    2. Maritain, Raïssa—Correspondence. 3. Tate, Allen,
    1899– —Correspondence. 4. Gordon, Caroline, 1895–
    —Correspondence. I. Dunaway, John M., 1945– .
    II. Maritain, Jacques, 1882–1973.   III. Series.
    B2430.M3A4   1992
    194—dc20   92-18979
                                          CIP

The paper in this book meets the guidelines for permanence and durability of the Committee on Production Guidelines for Book Longevity of the Council on Library Resources. ∞

B
2430
.M3H
A44
1992

This book is affectionately dedicated to my parents,
Marson Gale Dunaway, Jr.,
and
Kit Matteson Dunaway

CONTENTS

ILLUSTRATIONS

PREFACE

When I was writing a book on Jacques Maritain in the mid-seventies, I wrote letters to a list of American writers who I thought might have been influenced by Maritain. The responses were quite interesting, but none were so generous and enthusiastic as that of Caroline Gordon. Gordon wrote several pages, in which she spoke in glowing terms of what Maritain had meant to her personally, spiritually, and in her writing career. She enclosed a copy of a wonderful letter that Maritain had sent her after reading one of her novels, *The Malefactors* (1956), and encouraged me to keep in touch, saying she had in her possession other "material which I think will be helpful to you. It has not hitherto been accessible to the public."[1] I quoted from this letter—as well as a short one from Allen Tate—in my book *Jacques Maritain,* but as I continued to find interesting examples of Maritain's influence on American writers, a seed was planted in my mind. It was the germ of a project that I finally began to pursue in 1988 when I visited Antoinette Grunelius at the Cercle d'Etudes Jacques et Raïssa Maritain, in Kolbsheim, Alsace—namely, to compile and publish the letters between the Maritains and Allen Tate and Caroline Gordon, two remarkable Catholic literary couples.

Because of the relatively small number of letters gathered at the Maritain center and at the Princeton University Library, I opted to use all of them that were available. I also requested letters from the Jacques Maritain Center at the University of Notre Dame, but it had none. I believe there are relatively few extant letters missing from the collection gathered here. I have chosen to leave unusual spellings, punctuation, and headings, although I have corrected apparent typographical and proofreading errors in the originals. In reproducing undated letters, I refer in brackets to the postmark from the envelope if it was preserved with the letter. The absence or presence of diacritical marks (as in "Raissa" and "Raïssa") is also reproduced as in the original documents. Where the Maritains or a third party wrote in French, I have translated the original texts.[2] My

1. Caroline Gordon to editor, July 25, 1976, reprinted in Prologue.
2. The following letters are translated from the French: Nos. 25, 27, 61, 69, 74 (the second sentence only was written in English), 77, 80, and, in Appendix A, the letters from Jacques Maritain to Mgr. R. Fontenelle and from Sister Marie Pascale to Caroline Gordon.

translations of occasional French phrases and sentences in letters written otherwise in English appear in the notes.

Appendix A reproduces several notes and letters written by Maritain's secretaries and some letters from Maritain and Tate to third parties figuring prominently in certain discussions within the correspondence proper. Appendix B contains excerpts from an interview I conducted with Francis Fergusson on June 9, 1976, when I was gathering material for *Jacques Maritain*.

In the preparation of a book of letters, an editor is particularly dependent upon the services of others, and in this respect I feel fortunate indeed. In France, I was warmly greeted, efficiently served, and abundantly encouraged by Mme Grunelius and René Mougel, who directs the Maritain archives in Kolbsheim. In my own country I benefited from the kind services of the Princeton University Library staff, especially Jean Preston, Curator of Manuscripts, as well as Ralph McInerny and the staff of the Jacques Maritain Center at the University of Notre Dame. The Tate and Gordon heirs, Nancy Tate Wood and Helen Tate, were always helpful and gracious toward me, and I am grateful to Thomas Underwood, Walter Sullivan, Anthony Simon, Bernard Doering, and Deal Hudson for their encouragement and advice. Among the staff of the Mercer University Library, I am especially indebted to Valerie Edmonds, Virginia Cairns, Ann Park, and Mary Horton. I also wish to thank the American Maritain Association for permission to reprint the Introduction. Finally, I want to thank my wife Trish and our children, Michael, Jenny, and Joseph, for their enduring support and encouragement during this project.

EXILES AND FUGITIVES

INTRODUCTION

During the years of his American residence Jacques Maritain made some significant and lasting friendships, relationships that ultimately exerted a decisive influence on the history of thought and letters in this country. Among the more enduring such "grandes amitiés," if we may appropriate Raïssa Maritain's phrase from her 1941 memoir, was one the Maritains enjoyed with the poet Allen Tate and his first wife, novelist Caroline Gordon.[1]

It is often remarked that one of the greatest gifts with which Jacques Maritain was blessed was his genius for friendship. That his contacts ranged much farther than the worlds of philosophy and theology is an indication of the special nature of his calling as a "philosophe dans la cité." Knowing statesmen, poets, painters, priests, labor leaders, novelists, and musicians, Maritain strove to communicate with them in their own idiom in order to bring to bear on their diverse problems the fruitful perspectives of Thomistic wisdom.

The Maritains had a vision of making their home a "centre de rayonnement"—a center for a kind of sphere of spiritual influence—in the modern world for the timeless truths of Saint Thomas Aquinas' work. This vision was a guiding force in the forming of their friendships, especially at Meudon, a southwestern suburb of Paris where the Maritains owned a home during the height of the Renouveau catholique (Catholic Revival of Letters) in the 1920s and 1930s. It was also evident at Princeton, Notre Dame, Chicago, and the other American cities where the Maritains lived from 1940 to 1945, and again from 1948 to 1960, during their long exile from their beloved France.[2] One of the things that the Tates held in common with the Maritains was precisely the radiant hospitality that brought so many creative people to their homes. Benfolly, a farm overlooking the Cumberland River, was home not only to the Tates but, for varying periods of time, to Ford Madox Ford (and his wife, secretary, and sister-in-law), Robert Lowell (who showed up uninvited and pitched a tent on the lawn), and Katherine Anne Porter. Writers and art-

1. Raïssa Maritain, *Les Grandes Amitiés: Souvenirs* (New York, 1941).
2. From 1945 to 1948 Maritain served as French ambassador to the Vatican.

ists, especially those associated with the Agrarian movement, enjoyed the hospitality of the Tates throughout their marriage: the Robert Penn Warrens, the Malcolm Cowleys, the Mark Van Dorens, the Andrew Lytles, and others.

Both the Maritains and the Tates began their careers in literary renaissance groups that favored the wisdom of the ancients over the prophets of modern secularism. Indeed, the Renouveau catholique in France had certain sources in common with the Southern Renaissance in the United States, which began with the Fugitive poets in Tate's undergraduate days at Vanderbilt University. The richest flowering of southern literature probably owed as great a debt to Allen Tate as to any other single writer. His poetry and literary theory and criticism remain significant entries in the canon, and *The Fathers* (1938) is one of the most remarkable first novels in American literature. Although Caroline Gordon does not rank among the best-known fiction writers, she had an admirable gift for rendering detail and was a peculiarly insightful student and teacher of the craft of fiction. Readers of *The Southern Mandarins* will hardly be surprised to hear me call her a gifted epistolary stylist.[3]

The letters exchanged between the Maritains and the Tates reveal a rich tapestry of mutual respect, of intellectual fervor, and of constructive criticism. There is a lively flow of ideas and advice, as well as the kind of support and counsel that can only spring from deeply shared experience. Tate's letters are relatively few, with long spans in between, but testify to a genuine devotion to the French philosopher. Gordon's are more numerous, much longer, and more directly focused on Jacques Maritain's writings, as they impinge on her own thought and fiction. Jacques himself always writes as the wise counselor and affectionate encourager, Raïssa as the fellow poet, translator, and friend.

Tate has stated that "Jacques Maritain's influence on me was pervasive from the time I first knew him in 1940 until his death." Yet although the Maritains eventually became the godparents of Tate and Gordon, it seems unlikely that Maritain had a decisive role in Tate's conversion, shortly after that of his wife, to Roman Catholicism in the late 1940s. It is certainly clear that the southern writer—in the absence of religious training—had arrived at the point of decision through an intellectual route similar to that of Maritain, having long been an Aristotelian with a strong classical formation and preferring among modern poets such figures as T. S. Eliot and Charles Baudelaire. Walter Sullivan observes that

3. Sally Wood, ed., *The Southern Mandarins: Letters of Caroline Gordon to Sally Wood, 1924–1937* (Baton Rouge, 1984).

Tate was indeed predisposed toward the neo-Scholastic world view. So a meeting of like minds is more probable than an influence, although Francis Fergusson, who knew both the Tates and the Maritains during their Princeton years, has said that Tate came to read Aquinas through Maritain and that Tate's Thomism was a part of the French philosopher's influence. In fact, Fergusson maintained that Maritain was a major influence in bringing Tate to Catholicism.[4]

The earliest reference in the letters to a face-to-face meeting between the two couples is to 1949 in New York. The first exchange of letters—in 1944 between Jacques Maritain and Allen Tate—concerns Tate's request for an article for the *Sewanee Review*, of which he was editor in the mid-forties. Maritain responded by providing an excerpt from the recent translation of his *Réponse à Jean Cocteau* (1926), which was published as "The Double Heart" in the *Sewanee Review* that year.[5]

As the relationship matures, we read of Maritain asking Tate to critique an essay, especially in regard to his English usage, about which he was quite self-conscious. Gordon offers to take Raïssa Maritain for an automobile ride during one of Raïssa's extended recuperations. There is mention of a bill proposed in Congress in order to obtain a permanent visa for Raïssa's sister, Vera.[6] The bill is introduced by Congressman John F. Kennedy, and Tate enlists the support of Senator Robert Taft. In 1951 there is an exchange involving the Maritains' translation of Tate's "Ode to the Confederate Dead" into French. The French version was published in this country in the *Sewanee Review* and in France in *Le Figaro littéraire*.

One of the more interesting discussions in the correspondence concerns Tate's relationship to an organization of lay Catholics that included Frederick Morgan, editor of the *Hudson Review*, Robert Fitzgerald, the poet and translator, and others. In 1951 and 1952 a controversy developed over a motion picture called *The Miracle*, being shown in New York. Part of a Roberto Rossellini trilogy entitled *Ways of Love*, it is the story of an imbecilic peasant woman, Anna Magnani, who is seduced by a man she believes to be a saint. Francis Cardinal Spellman publicly condemned the film as blasphemous and insulting to Italian womanhood and

---

4. Allen Tate to editor, May 4, 1976, reprinted in Prologue; Walter Sullivan, *Allen Tate: A Recollection* (Baton Rouge, 1988), 70; Francis Fergusson, interview with editor, June 9, 1976, excerpted in Appendix B.

5. Jacques Maritain, "The Double Heart," *Sewanee Review*, LII (1944), 457–64.

6. Vera Oumansoff, Raïssa's sister, was a constant companion to the Maritains until her death in 1959. She was the Martha to Raïssa's Mary.

called for a boycott among Roman Catholics. Pickets, counterpickets, lawsuits, in short, a full-blown *cause célèbre* ensued, and the stream of articles in the New York *Times* during those months included a letter from Allen Tate. Apparently, the laymen's group was considering legal action against Cardinal Spellman in the affair, but Tate was instrumental in heading off this potentially divisive tactic. Maritain wrote to him—as well as Morgan—that the group would be more effective if it were "concerned with creative and constructive work, not with ecclesiastical politics." Tate wrote back that he fully agreed with Maritain. "My opinion from the beginning . . . was that we should form a Catholic literary academy, not a group for political action. . . . I agree with you that the only way to make works of imagination and sensibility a part of Catholic life is to produce enough of them, of sufficient power and distinction, [to] affect the education of the Catholic community as a whole, clergy as well as laity."[7]

Thus we find Maritain and Tate in accord on the ideal strategy for Catholic writers collectively to exert an effective influence on society. And Maritain supported Tate's individual public expression of opinion via the letter to the editor: "There is nothing in common between expressing one's mind on the matter, as you did, and starting a collective action which would raise the flag of a theologico-political crusade."[8]

This much can be learned from the correspondence. If we read Tate's letter to the New York *Times*, however, we discover another important aspect of this controversy in which the two are in apparent disagreement. In his letter to the editor, Tate argues that because of the separation of church and state there is no institution in this country with a "legitimate authority to suppress books and motion pictures, however disagreeable they may be to certain persons on theological grounds." He closes the letter by charging that "in the long run what Cardinal Spellman will have succeeded in doing is insulting the intelligence and faith of American Catholics with the assumption that a second-rate motion picture could in any way undermine their morals or shake their faith."[9]

The clear implication in this text is that Tate opposed censorship on any grounds, whether theological or moral. But his friend Jacques Maritain would never have taken such a position, judging from what he wrote in *The Responsibility of the Artist*. "When it comes to the *moral* or *im-*

7. Jacques Maritain to Allen Tate, February 27, 1952, No. 29 herein; Allen Tate to Jacques Maritain, March 2, 1952, No. 30 herein.
8. Jacques Maritain to Allen Tate, February 27, 1952, No. 29 herein.
9. New York *Times*, February 2, 1951, p. 24.

moral value of a literary work, the community may have to guard its standards against it to the extent that it is an *incitation to action*. . . . We cannot deny that people who are not specialists in literature have a right to be warned against reading authors whose artistic talent is but a means to unburden their vices and obsessions on us."[10]

Also of note is a 1954 letter from Maritain praising Caroline Gordon's story "Emmanuele! Emmanuele!" The principal character of the story, which appeared that year in the *Sewanee Review*, is easily recognizable to students of French literature as André Gide. Gide's stormy relationships with his wife, Madeleine Rondeaux, and with Paul Claudel are recreated here with what Maritain terms "such power of emotion, human compassion and generosity."[11] The stroke of genius in Gordon's treatment, however, is to entrust the narrative perspective to an otherwise minor character, an impressionable young professor and would-be poet who is hired as Gide's amanuensis. His adoring, awe-struck attitude toward the great writer is replete with bitter irony, somewhat reminiscent of the Curé de Luzarne's attitude toward Antoine Saint-Marin, Georges Bernanos' fictionalized version of Anatole France in *Sous le soleil de Satan* (1926). Indeed, the French Catholic novelist would have been pleased with Gordon's satirical treatment of the legendary Gide.

Perhaps the richest literary exchange is the one occasioned by the publication of *The Malefactors*, Gordon's 1956 novel, which carried as dedicatory epigraph a quote from Maritain's *The Frontiers of Poetry*. "Few books [have] moved me so deeply," wrote Maritain after reading the novel, "perhaps because I felt everywhere the vivid presence of your heart. This book is full of poetry, —implacable and loving, et d'un dessin admirablement sûr [and with an admirably assured design]. . . . But the great thing is the sense of the lovingkindness of Our Lord which permeates the entire book." Gordon was particularly gratified that Maritain was one of the relatively few readers to understand that although real people like Hart Crane, Dorothy Day, and Peter Maurin were recognizable in the characters of her story, they played a minor role in the *roman à clef*. "Maritain was the only critic who realized," she wrote in 1976, "that I had achieved what Ezra Pound years ago labelled 'an invention.' He also recognized the technique I used: adding an extra dimension to the 'literal level' (to borrow Dante's phrase.)" Several years later, on December 24, 1961, she enthusiastically mentions to Maritain an essay that

10. Jacques Maritain, *The Responsibility of the Artist* (New York, 1960), 79–80.
11. Jacques Maritain to Caroline Gordon, May 5, 1954, No. 37 herein.

takes these ideas as a point of departure. Ashley Brown's "The Novel As Christian Comedy" is one of the most creative interpretations that has been written on *The Malefactors*. It borrows liberally from Francis Fergusson's work on the *Purgatorio*, in addition to Maritain.[12]

The deep, enduring friendship between Flannery O'Connor and Caroline Gordon has been documented in *The Habit of Being* and in the critical commentaries published on the two writers. It is now widely acknowledged that Gordon was for many years O'Connor's principal mentor. There are several mentions of O'Connor's fiction in these letters, and we may infer that Maritain owed much of his familiarity with the author of *Wise Blood* to Gordon. In one letter to Maritain she encloses peacock feathers from O'Connor's farm in Georgia, Andalusia, and speaks of sending a photograph of Maritain to a Father Charles at the Trappist monastery in Conyers, Georgia. "Father Charles—originally one of the most dissolute young men who ever came Dorothy Day's way, she says—is a great admirer of yours and of Raïssa's and will be very happy to have it. These monks have sort of adopted Flannery O'Connor and me as pipe-lines to the outer world."[13]

Several years later, Gordon writes: "I have just finished a piece in which I tried to compare the last story in Flannery O'Connor's posthumous volume, *Everything That Rises Must Converge*, with the several versions of Flaubert's *Temptations de Saint Antoine* [*sic*]. It seems to me that Flannery succeeded where the great Flaubert failed, chiefly, because she confined herself to a portrayal of the operations of one heresy whereas Flaubert had nineteen or twenty parade past Saint Anthony."[14]

In two letters to Maritain in 1968 and 1969 Gordon speaks of Eugene McCarthy's presidential campaign. "We knew McCarthy and his wife in Minnesota. They are wonderful people. Gene is, doubtless, the best educated man in American politics. He is a devout Catholic—has taken St. Thomas More as his patron. Everybody says he can't possibly win. . . . But a good many people are beginning to realize that he is

---

12. Jacques Maritain to Caroline Gordon, March 28, 1956, No. 42 herein; Caroline Gordon to editor, July 25, 1976, reprinted in Prologue; Caroline Gordon to Jacques Maritain, December 24, 1961, No. 70 herein. See also Ashley Brown, "The Novel as Christian Comedy," in *Reality and Myth: Essays in American Literature in Honor of Richmond Croom Beatty*, ed. William E. Walker and Robert L. Welker (Nashville, 1964); Francis Fergusson, *Dante's Drama of the Mind: A Modern Reading* (Princeton, 1953).

13. Sally Fitzgerald, ed., *The Habit of Being: Letters of Flannery O'Connor* (New York, 1979), 260 *et passim;* Caroline Gordon to Jacques Maritain, December 24, 1961, No. 70 herein.

14. Caroline Gordon to Jacques Maritain, February 11, 1968, No. 76 herein.

attempting something that hasn't been attempted before. [You might almost say that he is creating a new political climate.]"[15] She even compares McCarthy's significance in America to that of the Little Brothers of Charles de Foucauld in France.[16]

At this time Gordon was beginning her third reading of Maritain's *The Peasant of the Garonne* (1967), about which she was extremely enthusiastic. She wrote Maritain that she told anyone who would listen that "if they want to understand their own times they had better read this book." The example she gives is a lengthy account of her daughter Nancy's dealings with McCarthy. Nancy Wood had worked hard in his presidential campaign and in the fall of 1969 was trying to help build the foundation for another McCarthy run at that office. Nancy ate lunch with McCarthy, and "their conversation, which lasted three hours, was mostly about angels—and angelism, she said. (At this point I was reminded of something you said in print years ago, that our chief danger was not from the atom bomb but from 'angelism,' man's effort to use his own intellect as if it were an angel's intellect.)" Gordon reports that McCarthy attributed Bobby Kennedy's opportunism in the campaign to his "succumb[ing] to the guidance of [his] dark angel."[17]

There are, of course, more personal notes in these letters from time to time, the most delicate of which concern Tate and Gordon's marital difficulties. The details, however, are so sketchy that there is practically no material for literary muckrakers. Maritain plays the role of peacemaker on occasion, but he has the wisdom to keep his interventions to a minimum. In March of 1957 Tate writes to thank him for his faithful support during the definitive break-up of the marriage. "Your letter has been like a beacon in the night—the compassion and charity which do not judge. I am deeply grateful, and send you-all my love." Maritain replies a few days later: "I was touched to the heart by your letter, —as I was also by my talk with Caroline. So deep a mutual love, and such suffering at the core of it!"[18]

Earlier I mentioned Maritain's vision of his home's becoming a "centre

15. Caroline Gordon to Jacques Maritain, March 12, 1968, No. 78 herein. The bracketed sentence is struck through in the typescript. Also see No. 79.

16. Charles Eugène, Vicomte de Foucauld (1858–1916) was a French ethnographer, linguist, military officer, explorer, and Christian mystic whose work in North Africa brought him the veneration of the Tuaregs, among whom he lived. The Little Brothers of Jesus is one of three religious orders founded on his rule of monastic life.

17. Caroline Gordon to Jacques Maritain, October 25, 1969, No. 79 herein.

18. Allen Tate to Jacques Maritain, March 8, 1957, No. 55 herein; Jacques Maritain to Allen Tate, March 21, 1957, No. 56 herein.

de rayonnement," where writers and artists would encounter the reality of divine grace and its energizing possibilities for them. That vision reappeared in a more generalized form near the end of Maritain's life in his concept of the "little flocks of the laity"—small study groups and social action groups that were to grow out of confessional community—which he hoped would exert a profound influence on modern culture.[19] The Tates were unable to operate together in such a way after the mid-1950s, but until then they indeed fulfilled many of Maritain's cherished goals. That they continued to work toward these goals individually after their final divorce is perhaps best evidenced in Gordon's plan to bequeath a portion of her papers to the Raïssa Maritain Library, run by the Sisters of the Sacred Heart, in Princeton, New Jersey. "One reason for leaving my stuff to the library at Stuart Hall is the chance that some earnest young writer may meet Mother Kirby or some of the other Sisters of the Sacred Heart and, consequently, have a little light thrown on his pathway." Later she remarks, "I hope the deposits will serve the purpose we both have at heart to lead people not of the faith to Raïssa who will, as you say, lead them to Christ."[20]

To a whole generation of American Catholics, Jacques Maritain was the foremost philosopher and theologian (even though he persistently refused the latter role himself). His importance to both Allen Tate and Caroline Gordon illustrated the position he commanded in American religious and intellectual circles in the two decades following the Second World War. The Maritains were even godparents to a considerable number of converts, American as well as French.

Allen Tate, Caroline Gordon, and Jacques and Raïssa Maritain devoted much of their careers to the renewal of modern culture in the West. A succinct expression of the essential hope for such a renewal is found in Gordon's letter to Maritain of May 7, 1954: "Allen is representing the United States at Mayor La Pira's Christian Congress in Florence. His speech will be largely his comments on your new book [*Creative Intuition in Art and Poetry*]: 'It will be just the right thing, for Jacques' theory of art boils down to the doctrine that Culture cannot survive without Revelation.' "[21]

19. The "little flocks of the laity" are described in Jacques Maritain, "The Spiritual Mission of the Laity," trans. Bernard E. Doering, *Communio*, XIV (Summer, 1987), 193–202.

20. Caroline Gordon to Jacques Maritain, November 2, 1964, September 29, 1965, Nos. 71, 75 herein, respectively.

21. Caroline Gordon to Jacques Maritain, May 7, 1954, No. 38 herein.

ALLEN TATE TO EDITOR

Running Knob Hollow Road
Sewanee, Tennessee 37375
May 4, 1976

Dear Mr. Dunaway:

Thank you for your letter. I wish I could encourage you to come to see me but the simple truth is that I have been bedridden with Emphyzema [*sic*] for over a year. Jacques Maritain's influence on me was pervasive from the time I first knew him in 1940 until his death. The nature of that influence you will find in some of my essays especially "The Symbolic Imagination" and "The Angelic Imagination." Perhaps the index of my *Essays of Four Decades* will give you other references. Jacques was a very great man. Not only a great intellect but a warm and friendly human being who had he been a clergyman would no doubt be canonized.

Sincerely yours,
Allen Tate

CAROLINE GORDON TO EDITOR

University of Dallas
Irving, Texas 75061
July 25, 1976

Dear Prof. Dunaway:

I am glad to have your letter. I will be eighty years old in October and at present am working (literally,) night and day to finish a novel I have had in progress twenty years or more. It is imperative that I finish this book this summer before the academic term starts in the Fall. If I don't I will not only throw away twenty years of hard labour but I will leave the body of my fiction without the perspective this book, the last piece of fiction I will write, gives it.[1]

I mention these facts so that you can understand my situation. Your project strikes me as the most worthwhile project that has come my way in many a year—perhaps in my whole lifetime. I will do anything I can to help you. I would be glad to talk with you at any time but I cannot take my nose from my own grindstone at present. Airplane travel is very expensive. I suggest that we confer by telephone. It will be expensive but not as expensive as airplane flights. I have material which I think will be helpful to you. It has not hitherto been accessible to the public.

I enclose a copy of a letter which Jacques Maritain wrote me on March 28, 1955.[2]

He had just had one of the first of a series of Coronary Occlusions. His doctor told a few friends that he was enough recovered to see a few friends and to do some light reading. I—like a fool—sent him a copy of my novel, *The Malefactors* as "light reading."

The book is dedicated to him and has a quotation from one of his early books: "It is for Adam to interpret the voices Eve hears."[3]

Jacques' extraordinary humility allowed all sorts of people to translate his early works. Later in life he had to ask permission from some of these translators to re-translate his own words. I forget whose translation I quote from.

One of the things that most impressed me about Jacques was that he read novels as if he were a novelist, read poetry as if he were a poet and looked at pictures as if he were a PAINTER. I can't express an opinion about his reactions to Music since I, myself, am "tone deaf" and, according to some musical friends, "tone dumb" as well.

The Malefactors had a bad press. Only a handful of reviewers seemed to have an inkling of what I was trying to do. Writing a novel—or a poem or a play, I gather—is an adventure for the author. He hardly knows what he is doing while he is in the act of creation. Maritain was the only critic who realized that I had achieved what Ezra Pound years ago labelled "an invention." He also recognized the technique I used: adding an extra dimension to the "literal level" (to borrow Dante's phrase.)

He also makes an important distinction in this letter, it seems to me, when he defines the nature of the *roman à clé*. Most readers have an erroneous conception of its nature.

Proust wrote forcefully on this subject to "one of his princesses." "Madame, I did not write you. I wrote about you." Henry James has treated the subject more explicitly than any other author when he refused to again receive a young novelist, Vernon Lee, who had satirized him in a novel. "I do not care to care," he wrote his fuss budget of a brother, William, who was all for "taking steps." "But I will not see her again.

She has committed two crimes. She has invaded my privacy and she has put a human being into a novel without re-imagining him."

Maritain knew more about the novel, I think, than any body I have ever known. One of his early books, *Art and Scholasticism*, contains what I consider the most profound and complete aesthetic of the novel. He wrote:

> Wherever art has attained a certain grandeur and purity, whether Hittite, Babylonian, Assyrian or Greek, it is already Christian—in hope.

My own most recent publication, *The Glory of Hera*, is based on this pronouncement. I always told Jacques that I followed—if remotely—in his wake.

I will dive into my (ill-kept) files and try to find some more of his letters. I suspect that his series of Coronaries were initially brought on by his efforts to learn English when he was in his sixties.

His later letters to me are in French. His English had left him.

He told me before he joined the "Little Brothers of Charles de Foucould" that he felt that that order was the most vital element in modern France.[4] You know, of course, that he was an ardent Nationalist and maintained that since France was "the eldest daughter of the Church" that she would do some great deed before the end of the world.

He was treated shamefully by Princeton University. During his stay there his salary was paid, not by the University, but by philanthropic Jewish persons. The head of the Philosophy department, "a Logical Positivist," urged him "not to give the boys so much Plato and Aristotle but more Bertrand Russell and Whitehead." He delivered the lectures which were finally published as *Creative Intuition* to a bunch of housewives. I, I am ashamed to say, was not of that number.

My telephone number is 214-438-7648.

My street address is

> 1730 East Northgate Drive, #1061,
> Irving, Texas, 75062

Two telephone companies are battling for control of the system here. . . . I don't get many of my calls. I am listed in the book as C. Gordon Tate. If you really want to talk with me you will have to persist. Many of my friends don't get through.

Again, I wish you all success in your project. In recent years I have been impressed by the fact that SO MANY OF Maritain's ideas are in circulation, without his name being mentioned.

Caroline Gordon

I am Miss Caroline Gordon—never *Ms*! In private life I am Mrs. Gordon Tate.[5]

These aliases are accidental, not from choice. I published my first novel as Caroline Gordon. Publishers don't want you to change names.

1. Gordon is referring to "The Joy of the Mountains," which was left unfinished and unpublished at her death. It concerned Meriwether Lewis (of Lewis and Clark fame), who was one of her ancestors.

2. No. 42 herein. The actual date of the letter was March 28, 1956.

3. Jacques Maritain, *The Frontiers of Poetry*, in *"Art and Scholasticism" and "The Frontiers of Poetry,"* trans. Joseph W. Evans (Notre Dame, Ind., 1974), 141.

4. See note 16 of the Introduction.

5. Unsure of Gordon's preference in titles, the editor had opted to address his letter to her as "Ms."

Allen Tate at his desk.
Courtesy Princeton University Libraries.

Caroline Gordon at the Red House in Princeton.
Courtesy Princeton University Libraries.

Allen Tate and Caroline Gordon in
their Perry Street apartment in New
York, *ca.* 1950.
Courtesy John Anderson Prince.

a
Merry Christmas
and a
Happy New Year

Caroline and Allen Tate
1949

The Tates' 1949 Christmas card, fea-
turing Benbrackets, their newly ac-
quired house in Princeton.
*From Van Wyck Brooks Collection,
Special Collections Dept., Van Pelt/
Dietrich Library, University of
Pennsylvania.*

The Red House, Ewing Street, Princeton, where Gordon wrote most of her lengthy letters to Maritain.
Photo by Gary Blackburn, courtesy Ann Waldron.

Jacques Maritain in his later years.
Copyright John Howard Griffin, courtesy Elizabeth Griffin-Bonazzi.

Raïssa Maritain in New York, 1944.
Courtesy Stuart Country Day School, Princeton.

The Maritains' house on Linden Lane in Princeton.
Photo by author.

The Raïssa Maritain Library, Stuart Country Day School, Princeton.
Courtesy Stuart Country Day School, Princeton.

1

ALLEN TATE TO JACQUES MARITAIN

The Library of Congress
Washington
Reference Department
April 13, 1944

Dear Jacques Maritain:

Beginning with the October 1944 issue I shall be the editor of *The Sewanee Review*, which I hope to resuscitate from an academic limbo and wake into a dynamic force. I should like tremendously the honor of printing an essay by you in my first issue. Could you not find time to write something for me on the relation of Christianity to contemporary literature? Or if some other theme is uppermost in your mind, I should like that too.—I must add that hitherto the *Review* has not paid for material, but that I shall be able to pay one cent a word.

If you come to Washington I hope you will give me the pleasure of seeing you.

Most sincerely yours,
Allen Tate

2

JACQUES MARITAIN TO ALLEN TATE

30 Fifth Avenue
New York 11, N.Y.
April 15, 1944

Dear Allen Tate:

I thank you most cordially for your kind letter. I consider it a great privilege to me to collaborate with you and I shall be delighted to contribute to *The Sewanee Review*. I am now so overwhelmed with harrying tasks that I wonder whether I can find the possibility to concentrate on the questions I love most, and to write you an essay for October. But do you think that an excerpt of an unpublished translation of my Letter to Jean Cocteau would be satisfactory to you?[1] One of my friends has just completed the translation of this Letter, and it seems to me it answers very well the subject you have in mind. If you approve of the idea I could send you the whole letter, and you could choose in it whatever would be most suitable for your review.

Of course it will give me great pleasure to see you if I go to Washington.

> With my best regards,
> Most sincerely yours,
> Jacques Maritain

1. Cocteau's *Lettre à Jacques Maritain* and Maritain's *Réponse à Jean Cocteau* were published together in Paris by Stock in 1927.

3

JACQUES MARITAIN TO ALLEN TATE

> 30 Fifth Avenue
> New York 11, N.Y.
> June 6, 1944

Dear Allen Tate:

Thank you very much for your letter of May 31; I am extremely sorry to have missed seeing you when you were in town. Please forgive my not having answered you right away, but my whole time was taken up by end-of-year work at the Ecole Libre des Hautes Etudes (I have resigned as president because that administrative position took away my freedom of mind).[1] I shall send you in a few days the excerpt from my *Letter to Jean Cocteau* which you might be interested in.

> With my kind regards,
> Yours sincerely,
> Jacques Maritain

1. The Ecole Libre des Hautes Etudes was a French university organized in New York by French exiles during World War II.

———————————————————— 4 ————————————————————

JACQUES MARITAIN TO ALLEN TATE

30 Fifth Avenue
New York 11, N.Y.
June 14, 1944

Dear Allen Tate:

I am sending you with this letter the excerpt from my ANSWER TO JEAN COCTEAU, which I promised you a few weeks ago. I hope you will find it suitable for *The Sewanee Review*. The translation—which is by one of my friends—is one of which I am highly satisfied.

Yours cordially,
Jacques Maritain

———————————————————— 5 ————————————————————

JACQUES MARITAIN TO ALLEN TATE

30 Fifth Avenue
New York 11, N.Y.
June 19, 1944

Dear Allen Tate:

Thank you very much for your kind letter, I am very happy that you are pleased with this essay.

The French title of the book is *Réponse à Jean Cocteau*. When he turned toward religious faith and wanted to make his conversion known, Cocteau wrote a *Lettre à Jacques Maritain*. His *Letter* and my *Answer* form two small separate books, which were published together as one single volume, in 1927. You know that Cocteau's conversion has not been a perfectly secure and lasting one.

John Coleman translated the two books.[1] But I hesitate greatly to publish them now, both because of the copyright which belongs to the French publisher and partly to Cocteau himself, and because I am very much concerned with the present attitude of Cocteau,—I should not like to have a book by him published before he has cleared himself, if it is possible, of the accusations of the French underground.

May I ask you to be so kind as to send me the proofs of the article, I wonder whether I shall not suppress the last paragraph or add something to it. For Cocteau was not faithful to that true freedom of which Father Charles Henrion spoke.[2]

With my kindest regards,

As ever yours,
Jacques Maritain

As for the title of my article in the magazine, I would suggest "God and Poetry" with a footnote explaining this is an extract from a small book "Answer to Jean Cocteau" published in Paris in 1926.[3]

1. They were eventually published as *Art and Faith: Letters Between Jacques Maritain and Jean Cocteau*, trans. John Coleman (New York, 1948).

2. Cocteau met Father Henrion at the Maritains' home in Meudon.

3. Maritain's *Réponse à Jean Cocteau* first appeared separately in 1926 before publication under the same cover with Cocteau's *Lettre à Jacques Maritain* in 1927.

6

JACQUES MARITAIN TO ALLEN TATE

New York
April 20, 1949

Dear Allen Tate,

We planned to see you and Mrs. Tate before leaving and we are terribly sorry to have been prevented from doing so. Raissa has been ill for more than two months, and that sickness has upset all our projects. Finally we are to sail tomorrow morning on the De Grasse, while she is just a convalescent, and it was impossible for us to see our friends as we would have liked. We shall be back in September, I hope that next year we shall have the great pleasure of seeing you more often. I bring with me your book which I admire very much, and I shall re-read it in France.[1] To Mrs. Tate and yourself all our good wishes and cordial regards.

Yours faithfully,
Jacques Maritain

1. This is probably Allen Tate, *The Hovering Fly & Other Essays* (Cumington, Mass., 1949).

7

JACQUES MARITAIN TO ALLEN TATE

Princeton, N.J.
26 Linden Lane
November 13, 49

Dear Allen Tate:

Would you make us the great pleasure of coming with Mrs. Tate and dining with us on Friday, November 18 at 7 o'clock? We will be alone and can speak at leisure.

A bientôt, I hope. With warmest regards to you both,

Yours faithfully,
Jacques Maritain

8

JACQUES MARITAIN TO ALLEN TATE

Thursday

Dear Allen:

I think that the road is *nature,* with all events and ventures we meet with on the way, and that the clear stream is *grace,* which runs all along nature and makes of all events and ventures divine opportunities.

It was good to see you both.

Love,
Jacques

9

CAROLINE GORDON TO JACQUES AND RAÏSSA MARITAIN

108 Perry Street
New York 14
November 28, 1949

Dear Mr. and Mrs. Maritain:

My husband and I regret that we are not living in Princeton this year, as we would like very much to see you again.[1] We are wondering whether you come to New York often and wondering, too, whether it would be possible for you to dine with us one evening?

Allen teaches at NYU on Tuesday and Wednesday evenings and I am at Columbia on Thursday evenings, but we try to keep all other evenings free, and there is, of course, Sunday when none of us are working. If you ever have any free time when you are in New York it would make us very happy if you could arrange to see us. There are so many things we want to talk to you about,

Sincerely yours,
Caroline Gordon Tate[2]

1. The Tates lived in the apartment at 108 Perry Street in New York through the fall of 1949, when they purchased the house they called Benbrackets at 465 Nassau Street in Princeton. They lived there until Tate was hired by the University of Minnesota in the fall of 1951. Maritain taught at Princeton from 1948 to 1960.

2. Some time after receiving this letter, Maritain wrote at the top of the page the text of a telegram addressed to the Tates, as follows: "Could you come and dine with us Friday 17 instead of Monday 20. Kindest regards. Maritain."

--------------------------------- 10 ---------------------------------

ALLEN TATE TO RAÏSSA MARITAIN

465 Nassau Street
Princeton, New Jersey
December 12, 1949

My dear Raissa Maritain:

Both Caroline and I are deeply grateful for your kindness in sending us *Lettre de Nuit—La Vie Donnée.*[1] We have been trying in our halting French to read the poems aloud, in the hope that we should thus receive the full richness of the diction. The deep sincerity of feeling and the distinction of mind do come through to us, and we are very much moved, particularly by two poems: En Esprit En Verite and La Croix du Sud, which seem to us very beautiful.

This is a precious gift, for which we shall always be grateful.

Sincerely yours,
Allen Tate

1. Raïssa Maritain, *Lettre de nuit, La Vie donnée* (Montreal, 1943), a collection of poems.

11

JACQUES MARITAIN TO ALLEN TATE

February 23, 1950
26 Linden Lane

Dear Allen,

Please excuse me for infringing upon your time! I just wrote in a hurry a paper for *Partisan Review*, I am enclosing it.[1] Would you be so kind as to read it? First I need your judgment, in order to know if it is worth publication. If you think that it does not help in the issue, tell me, I shall drop it gladly. Second, and supposing that you advise to publish, you will perhaps have the charity of correcting my awkward English. Then I would give the corrected manuscript to be typed, and send it to the review. A thousand thanks in advance!

> To you both our affectionate
> regards,
>   Yours faithfully,
>   Jacques

1. Maritain was a contributor to a symposium entitled "Religion and the Intellectuals," which was published in the *Partisan Review*, IX (April, 1950), 93–98. Tate also wrote a statement for that issue, which appears on 133–36.

12

JACQUES MARITAIN TO ALLEN TATE

April 18, 1950
26 Linden Lane

Dear Allen,

I vainly tried to get you on the telephone Sunday and yesterday, so I am writing these few lines to beg you to thank Mrs. Tate for us and to tell her how deeply Raïssa has been touched by her flowers. They were for her a touch of spring and a dear token of affection which have comforted her. She is eager to tell you both how grateful she is.

We had six atrocious weeks, that kind of shingles was the worst the doctor has ever seen. You know how painful it is. She is only beginning to feel better, we shall be unable to leave for France in May, we hope that this will be possible in June.

>Pray for us. Love to both of you.
>Jacques

13

CAROLINE GORDON TO JACQUES MARITAIN

>465 Nassau Street
>Princeton, New Jersey
>21 avril 50[1]

Dear Mr. Maritain:

Allen has been working over-time, finishing a piece of work and we have not gone anywhere or seen anybody for weeks and so did not know until just the other day that Mrs. Maritain was so ill! Do you not think that driving about a little in the spring air might be good for her when she gets a little better? We would like so much to take her for a drive any time she might want to go. We are here in Princeton every day of the week except Wednesdays and Thursdays. If a sunny day comes when she feels like a drive please telephone and let us know. In the meantime, our love to you both,

>Caroline

1. This letter was dated, apparently, by Maritain upon receipt, in accord with the post-mark on the envelope.

14

CAROLINE GORDON TO RAÏSSA MARITAIN

>465 Nassau Street
>Princeton, New Jersey
>Monday [postmarked November 7, 1950]

Dear Madame Maritain:

We are wondering whether you and Monsieur Maritain and Mademoiselle Oumandzov [*sic*] can come to tea on Friday afternoon at half past four or five o'clock?[1] Dorothy Day will be visiting us then and I know she would like so much to see all three of you.[2] We, too, have wanted very much to see you, but have been virtually *incommunicado* for two months, with this wretched building on of an addition. It is practically finished now and we can begin to live again. We do hope you can come on Friday,

Sincerely yours,
Caroline Tate

1. See note 6 of the Introduction.
2. Dorothy Day (1897–1980) was cofounder, with Peter Maurin, of the Catholic Worker movement in the 1930s. See note 4 of No. 42.

15

JACQUES MARITAIN TO ALLEN TATE

Princeton, N.J.
26 Linden Lane
November 20, 1950

Dear Allen:

Are you free Thursday, and could you come with Caroline for tea at 4:30? We would keep Thanksgiving together.

I shall try to telephone you today or tomorrow.

Love to both of you
Jacques

16

ALLEN TATE TO RAÏSSA MARITAIN

465 Nassau Street
Princeton
December 17, 1950

Dear Raïssa:

When we saw Jacques this morning he asked if you could come to my baptism! I had assumed, of course, that my provincial Southern "you all" (meaning *both of you*) would convey to Jacques my wish; but I should not have assumed it. It will make me very happy if you will come. And I hope that your sister will come too.

Sincerely yours,
Allen Tate

17

CAROLINE GORDON TO RAÏSSA MARITAIN

Monday [postmarked
December 18, 1950]

Dear Raissa:

I cannot tell you how happy I am that you and Jacques are to be Allen's god-parents—for I feel sure you won't refuse his request. He was so excited the other night that he thought Jacques' assent was for both of you.

My daughter and her husband are coming on Thursday, to stay until the next Monday.[1] I am wondering if you and Jacques and your sister could lunch or dine with us on Saturday of this week? I know that this is a very busy time and almost hate to ask you to consider another engagement. But if it is possible for you to come it would make us very happy. We are anxious for our children to have an opportunity to talk with you. Nancy's brief meeting with Jacques the other morning meant a great deal to her,

affectionately,
Caroline

1. Caroline Gordon and Allen Tate had one child, Nancy Tate, born in 1925. Her husband's name is Percy Wood.

—————————————— 18 ——————————————

CAROLINE GORDON TO RAÏSSA MARITAIN

465 Nassau Street
Princeton, New Jersey
Tuesday [postmarked December 27,
1950]

Dear Raissa:

Nancy was so happy to have the rosary as a gift from you—but she will be writing you herself.

They left yesterday in the midst of a snow storm. Both Nancy and Percy said that this was the happiest Christmas they had ever spent, and Allen and I felt the same way. The anxiety that we still feel about Percy's health was somehow suspended and we were all able to participate in the joys of Christmas.

You and Jacques and Vera did a great deal to bring that about. We thank all three of you and we send you our heartfelt good wishes for the new year,

With love,
Caroline

—————————————— 19 ——————————————

CAROLINE GORDON TO RAÏSSA MARITAIN

465 Nassau Street
Princeton, New Jersey
Friday [postmarked February 3,
1951]

Dear Raïssa:

We have two friends from Tennessee visiting us, the novelist, Brainard Cheney and his wife. Brainard Cheney is on the point of coming into the Church—we think—and would like above all things to meet you and Jacques. If you and Jacques and Vera can come to us for cocktails at five on Sunday it will make us very happy. But we realize that Jacques is working unusually hard now. If you can't come, please don't trouble to write or telephone. Just come if you can!

I saw Francis Fergusson this afternoon and he gave a glowing report of the second seminar. We regret more than ever that we are obliged to be in New York on Sundays, but I suppose the lectures will find their way into a book finally.

I finished my novel day before yesterday.[1] Now poor Allen has to read it and tell me what is wrong with it.

We still have had no final word about our son in law's condition. He has entered a competitive examination for young doctors, to get a job for next year and doesn't want to take the physical examination for that, with fresh scars on his neck, so has delayed the second examination he will have to have eventually. However, he has gained weight recently, which seems a good sign and a friend of ours, who is eminent in that field, tells us that he doesn't think the doctor concerned would have let him put the second examination off this long if he thought he had Hodgkins' Disease. Nancy and Percy are both rather dramatic young people, too. We can only hope that they have been needlessly alarmed.

Our love to you all,
Caroline

1. Caroline Gordon, *The Strange Children* (New York, 1951).

20

CAROLINE GORDON TO RAÏSSA MARITAIN

465 Nassau Street
Princeton, New Jersey
Tuesday [postmarked March 13, 1951]

Dear Raïssa:

How kind of you to send us LES DONS DU SAINT-ESPRIT! We are very happy to have it—and in your translation![1] Allen has just finished reading Julien Green's novel—and thinks it's extremely good.[2] Jean de Saint-Thomas will come next.

We heard that you and Vera have had the flu. I do hope you are recovered by this time. We had two light cases—me and Baby Allen. He recovered almost immediately. I am just beginning to feel like myself again.

The Woods are with us now and will stay here until Percy goes to his new job. Nancy and Percy will be baptized next Friday—March 16—at three o'clock in the parish church by Father Henry. We hope so much that you and Vera and Jacques can come and hope, too, that you can come to our house for tea later. But for Heaven's sake, don't come unless you are feeling up to it. The children will understand that you are with them in spirit. They have been wanting to come and call on you but thought they would wait until you were quite recovered. This is such a ghastly time of year! Almost everybody is ill with something or other.

I am one of the luckiest of mortals, though. Nancy and Percy set four different dates for their arrival. Each time they changed the date it was as if they had given my Muse a shot in the arm. I pictured Peto and Baby Allen speeding towards me at sixty miles an hour—their father is a fast driver—and I knew that I would never get my novel finished if I didn't finish it before they got here.[3] I finished the day before they arrived.

We have heard nothing but praises—and praises of the most glowing—of Jacques' seminars. I should think they must have taken a tremendous effort. You must all be glad that they are over—though he doubtless just goes from them to another tremendous effort!

We look forward to seeing you soon, and we do hope that you are feeling yourself again—you and Vera, too. All of us send our love, and many thanks for the book, which we will prize,

Caroline

1. *Les Dons du Saint-Esprit: Traité de Jean de Saint-Thomas*, trans. Raïssa Maritain (Paris, 1921).
2. Julian Green (1900—), a French novelist of American parentage, was one of Maritain's closest friends. Gordon is probably referring to his novel *Moïra*, trans. Denise Folliot (New York, 1951). She uses the French spelling of Green's first name, as did Tate.
3. The Woods had four children: Percy III (1944), Allen Tate (1947), Caroline (1952), and Amelia (1957).

21

CAROLINE GORDON TO RAÏSSA MARITAIN

465 Nassau Street
Princeton, New Jersey
Sunday [postmarked April 9, 1951]

Dear Raïssa:

When I first saw the notices of your LES GRANDES AMITIES I told myself that there was a book I wanted to read, and here I am, just getting to it because you have given it to the children.

It is a beautiful baptism gift for them. They revere you and Jacques so that they are fascinated to find you pictured as being as young in the life of grace as they are now. Allen and I, who are almost as young as they— I shall never get over wondering what we did with the first fifty years of our lives!—Allen and I are just as much fascinated by the book as they are.

I am so busy just now with household chores that I have little time to read and less time to write. In this hurried note I cannot attempt to tell you what the book has meant to me—the books, I should say, for I have had to read it in translation.[1] The incidents you present are absorbingly interesting, but they are illuminating, too, for the story you are chiefly concerned with is that of the life of grace, no matter in whose heart it is lived. In this story, which forms the gloss on all the other stories, you tell me many things I didn't know. I shall re-read your book often.

We often feel sorry for you and Jacques and Vera in your exile, for it is certainly an exile to have to live in a strange land, but it may console you when you reflect that your exile enriches many lives,

with love,
Caroline

It *is* astonishing when one reflects what influence a book can have. All the young people in Memphis, Tennessee will shortly be reading your book! If you knew Memphis, Tennessee as well as I do you'd be amused!

1. *Les Grandes Amitiés: Souvenirs* (1941) was translated by Julie Kernan and published under the title *We Have Been Friends Together* (New York, 1942).

22

JACQUES MARITAIN TO ALLEN TATE

26 Linden Lane
Princeton, N.J.
April 11, 1951

Dear Allen,

Thank you ever so much for having gotten Senator Taft's support! Please convey my best thanks to your brother.

I just received a letter of Congressman John F. Kennedy (a friend of Bishop Wright) telling me he has introduced a bill in behalf of Vera in the House of Representatives (H.R. 3567).[1] What kind of development is to follow remains deep mystery for my ignorance of legislative machinery.

Tell Caroline that Raissa treasures her letter and is so happy with it. Ah, when shall we be able to visit with you, some day, Memphis, Tennessee!

I am leaving in a few days for Notre Dame University, for some lectures. I am eager to see you when I am back.

Love to all of you,
Jacques

1. This was necessary to obtain a permanent visa for Vera.

23

JACQUES MARITAIN TO ALLEN TATE

26 Linden Lane
November 13, 1951

Dear Allen:

Pardon me for answering so late. I was completely overwhelmed by work and people in Chicago, and now in Princeton belated work and courses to prepare make me mad.[1] You know how deeply we miss you both. I envy the *power of words*,—why can I not be magically carried to Minneapolis and spend a day with you?[2] Yet it is good to know that you like the place and the people, and even the University. I was not aware that you had an Abbey in the vicinity. This experience of the unique presence of the Church everywhere is something celestial. May the monks love poetry as much as you love liturgy.

John Ransom sent me his Plan at the end of October, I had already seen Hutchins and unfortunately I could not meet him again.[3] I suppose that Ransom sent you a copy of the Plan. I find it very good, except on some points (there are mistakes in a paragraph about the Collège de France;—I doubt it is prudent to envisage right now [a] special building and dormitory for the school;—it seems to me that the Plan should be more concrete, especially with regard to the people who would teach there.)[4] I have returned the Plan to Ransom, so that he might change the passage about the Collège de France, and I have suggested to him to send it directly to Hutchins (that's surely the best way) in writing Hutchins that we discussed the question in Princeton and that I would surely have given the Plan to him in Chicago if I had received it earlier. I also told Ransom that I know now of the existence of three similar confidential plans which are inspired by the same general idea, that I am completely devoted to the idea, but that, as anxious as I am to have his Plan succeed, I don't think it is possible to endorse one plan in particular to the exclusion of others, under present fluid circumstances. It would rather be desirable that all of them could be brought into existence, though I doubt that one might find as many competent people as would be necessary for that. I shall keep you informed of the continuation of the story, as far as I know it.

I had not the time to see Herbert Read.[5] Jean de Menasce's Seminar will begin the day after tomorrow.[6] We are happy to have him here, he is wonderful. We are so sorry that he cannot see you. But perhaps it will be possible if you come over a little before Christmas? In any case I hope that he will return next year (he is seduced by America) and that he will then visit the big West, that is, Minneapolis.

We have finished the translation of the Ode to the Confederate Dead, and shall send it to you when Vera has typed it.

I shall write some lines (I have not read the Sewanee Review for many months) for John Palmer, as soon as I can.[7]

The bill in behalf of Vera has been passed by the Congress.

We hope to see Percy and Nancy Sunday.

Dear Allen, pray for us. We think every day of Caroline and you with profound affection. Raissa, Vera and I send our love to you both.

As ever yours,

Jacques

1. Maritain's English here should be corrected to read, "drive me mad."

2. "The Power of Words" was an essay written by Edgar Allan Poe in 1845, which Tate found useful in his own essay "The Angelic Imagination: Poe as God" (*Collected Essays* [New York, 1959], 432–54). Tate had been hired to teach writing at the University of Minnesota.

3. John Crowe Ransom (1888–1974) was a poet and critic and leader of the Agrarian movement at Vanderbilt; he was also the founder of the New Criticism. The "Plan" presumably had to do with the Great Books movement in higher education. Robert Maynard Hutchins (1899–1977) was president of the University of Chicago (1929–45) and one of the driving forces in the creation of the Great Books program there.

4. Established in 1529 by Francis I, the Collège de France is independent of the Sorbonne. Many free public lectures have been sponsored there, among them Henri Bergson's series, which counted heavily in Maritain's early formation.

5. Herbert Edward Read (1893–1968) was a British poet, essayist, art critic, and friend of T. S. Eliot. He was influenced by Maritain's writings.

6. Jean-Pierre de Menasce was a friend of the Maritains and a specialist in Iranian religion.

7. John E. Palmer was editor of the *Sewanee Review* from 1946 to 1952, between Tate and Monroe Spears.

24

ALLEN TATE TO JACQUES MARITAIN

1801 University Avenue Southeast
Minneapolis 14, Minnesota

Dear Jacques,

I was delighted to get your good letter of November 13. Day before yesterday I received from John Ransom the statement that he had doubtless sent you; it had not been revised in the light of your suggestions. I immediately wrote John that I agreed with your two points: that the names of the persons who would be expected to teach in the Institute should be included, and that all mention of a building for the Institute should be omitted. I am sure that John will accept your criticism. But alas, I fear that all this delay will prove to be fatal. John is now doing at the end of November what might have been accomplished at the end of September. The three competing plans are an ominous sign. I have no doubt that one or even all of them will be set forth in the approved educational jargon of "areas" etc., and that the more urbane language of John Ransom will seem to the Foundation bureaucrats hopelessly "inefficient". But so be it; I should not want it otherwise.

I am looking forward most eagerly to seeing the translation of my Ode, and I hope that Vera will have time soon to copy it. The translation by Jean Paulhan and Henry Church was accurate enough, but if the poem has any poetry in it, their translation seemed to omit it. A good many of my poems have been done into French, Italian, and Spanish, but never by persons of distinguished gifts. It is a great pleasure just to know that you and Raïssa thought enough of the poem to undertake the translation.

We miss you all more acutely all the time, and our loss is not in the least dulled by the very real pleasure that we feel in our new associations. We miss our children too—even the *noise* of the little boys. We were counting on seeing you in June, but now that Vera's difficulties are removed—we are very happy about this—you will all no doubt sail for France in May.

Francis writes me that you have agreed to write an essay for the Dante issue of The Kenyon Review.[1] My own poor essay will be in such high company that it will hang its head in shame.[2] Your views on Dante will appear with dramatic force; for many persons of my acquaintance have hoped that you might some time write about him.

We hope that all three of you will pray for us, and include a special intention for our speedy reunion. Caroline joins me in love to you all.

Affectionately yours,
Allen

1. Francis Fergusson (1904–86) was a teacher and writer whom the Maritains and Tates knew well during their Princeton years. He is author of *The Idea of a Theater* (Princeton, 1949) and *Dante's Drama of the Mind: A Modern Reading* (Princeton, 1953). Fergusson was "special editor" of the Dante number of the *Kenyon Review* (Spring, 1952), a wonderfully rich edition with articles by T. S. Eliot, R. P. Blackmur, Charles Singleton, and others. Maritain's essay for that issue, "Dante's Innocence and Luck," later became the last chapter of his book *Creative Intuition in Art and Poetry* (New York, 1953). Appendix B contains notes from the editor's interview with Fergusson on Maritain's relationship with Tate.

2. Allen Tate, "The Symbolic Imagination: A Meditation on Dante's Three Mirrors," *Kenyon Review,* XIV (Spring, 1952), 256–77.

—————— 25 ——————

RAÏSSA MARITAIN TO ALLEN TATE

Princeton
25 November 1951

Dear Allen,

Here is our translation of *Ode to the Confederate Dead*.[1] Jacques and I have worked on it not with ease but with joy, grasping better and better, as we tried to put your language into ours, the worth and beauty of your great poem.

Our joy is fragile, however, while it awaits your decision. If you find the translation accurate and readable in French we will be extremely happy.

We miss you and Caroline a great deal. Your presence and friendship helped us so much in our isolation. Jacques, Vera, and I think of you with all our hearts and send you our most affectionate remembrances.

Yours
Raïssa

P.S. There is even a footnote in the copy that I'm sending you. It is for French readers . . .

1. The translation was first published in *Le Figaro littéraire* (Paris), May 24, 1952, then in the *Sewanee Review*, LX (Summer, 1952), 512–17, and in LXI (1953), 2–7, with corrections.

26

ALLEN TATE TO RAÏSSA MARITAIN

1801 University Avenue Southeast
Minneapolis 14, Minnesota
November 28, 1951

My dear Raïssa:

Your translation and your very sweet note arrived late yesterday just as some people were gathering here for tea: I fear I was a poor host, for I withdrew to read the translation. But I finally brought it in to the company and asked a bi-lingual friend who was present to read it aloud. It had an electrifying effect. My jubilation turned somewhat to sadness when I began to suspect that the translation may be better than the original!

I am lost in admiration of the subtle combination of literal accuracy with an almost exact reproduction of the *rhythms* of the English. I simply do not understand how you and Jacques achieved this most difficult feat of translation. If I were citing examples of this, I should have to quote the entire translation. I am looking now at one beautiful instance of it—the transition from *N'entends rien que le vent* to *Maintenant que le sel de leur sang / Raidit les oubliettes plus salées de la mer*[1]—which renders not only the meaning quite perfectly, but the exact rhythm.

There is a single word that I might question, but I do not know enough to question it with any conviction. I refer to *optimistes* on page 4.

Shall we, more hopeful,
Set up the grave in the house?

"More hopeful" has some of the connotation of Hope, the theological virtue, rather than of optimism as opposed to pessimism. What I am saying, I suppose, is that in this passage Christian Hope, based upon Faith in the after-life, is ironically perverted into a cult of death. But you will know better than I how this idea should be rendered into the French. You will have already considered this question, I am sure.

I should feel greatly honored if you and Jacques decided to publish the translation. I am sure that any of a number of literary magazines would publish it in this country, perhaps along with the English text.

We miss the Maritains more and more, and not a day passes that we do not speak of all three of you with the greatest affection. Our love to you all.

Affectionately yours,
Allen

1. "Hears the wind only. / Now that the salt of their blood / Stiffens the saltier oblivion of the sea."

27

RAÏSSA MARITAIN TO ALLEN TATE

9 December 1951

Dear Allen,

You cannot imagine the joy your letter gives us. We are delighted—and very proud—that you like the translation of your great Ode. You might have found our enterprise presumptuous, and we were afraid of hurting you by hurting poetry. Now we are breathing in peace.

In translating *more hopeful*, by "plus optimiste" we intended to render better in French the underlying irony of the expression. But you are right, the word seems only to mean the opposite of pessimism, and abandons the connotations that you had envisioned. We think *Avec plus d'espérance* (with more hope) will be much better:

A la tombe? Avec plus d'espérance installerons-nous la tombe
   Dans la maison? La tombe rapace?

Yes, we would be very happy for an American literary journal to publish our work with the original text. It will be a contribution to the problem of the translation of poetry! What do you advise in this regard?

We saw Percy and Nancy; Nancy looks very good. She did not leave us hope that you and Caroline were coming to Princeton for Christmas. Will we see you here in spring or in France next summer? Vera got her permanent visa law. We hope to be able to go to France in June.

To Caroline, to you, dear Allen, all the affection of the three of us.

Yours,
Raïssa [1]

1. Among the letters at the Cercle d'Etudes Jacques et Raïssa Maritain there is a clipping from the May 24, 1952, issue of *Le Figaro littéraire*. It contains excerpts from "Ode aux morts confédérés" under the headline, "Allen Tate est à Paris." This undated note is written in the margin of the clipping: "Dear Raïssa and Jacques: M. Brisson [editor of *Le Figaro*] didn't include all of it, but nonetheless it is very nice. I have received many congratulations on it. A letter in a few days. Love, Allen."

28

ALLEN TATE TO RAÏSSA MARITAIN

1801 University Avenue Southeast
Minneapolis 14, Minnesota
December 14, 1951

My dear Raïssa:

Thank you so much for your letter of December 9. *Avec plus d'espérance* I am sure renders exactly the intentions of *more hopeful*. So now the translation is perfect! I have sent a copy to the editor of *The Sewanee Review*, suggesting that he publish it along with the English text, and perhaps with a brief commentary by Jackson Mathews, whose recent studies of Anglo-French translations have been very illuminating. [1]

Alas, we shall not be in Princeton until the end of June, and shall miss you. And we had to give up our plans for a European trip. The Income Tax people recently informed me that I owed a vast sum (vast for me) on my 1946 tax! So for a while we shall probably be begging our bread from door to door! But we shall see you in September.

When I hear from Mr. Palmer (of The Sewanee Review) I will let you know. Meanwhile we are delighted by the good news of Vera's visa; and send love to all three of you.

Affectionately yours,
Allen

1. Jackson Mathews (*ca.* 1907–78) was an educator, poet, and translator of Gide, Baudelaire, and Valéry. His translation of Valéry's *La Soirée avec M. Teste* won the National Book Award in 1974.

JACQUES MARITAIN TO ALLEN TATE

Princeton, N.J.
February 27, 1952

My dear Allen:

I enclose a copy of my answer to a kind letter of Mr. Morgan, which was of great interest—and concern—for me, and which obliged me to tell him bluntly my thought about his project.[1] I think that the group of which he speaks might do a remarkable job but on the condition that it set off on another track, and be concerned with creative and constructive work, not with ecclesiastical politics. This goes exceedingly farther than the question of the *Miracle*.[2] Moreover, there is nothing in common between expressing one's mind on the matter, as you did, and starting a collective action which would raise the flag of a theologico-political crusade. The confusions and misunderstandings thus engendered would jeopardize from the start all the good that such a group is capable of doing.

I am optimistic as to the future of American Catholicism, but what worries us in its present situation results from deep-rooted historical circumstances and will improve only by having new seeds germinate and take root. That's why I am afraid of any possible mistake,—such as the attitude pointed at in Morgan's letter would be. I also have a strong feeling of the kind of isolation in which writers and artists are in this country.

I am terribly sorry not to be able to speak of all these things with you. I beg you to supplement what is perhaps insufficiently clarified in my letter to Morgan, and to understand what kind of long and difficult task is required in my opinion, a task quite humble with respect to men but not humble at all with respect to creative work.

Given your deep authority on American writers, your guidance will be decisive. But it is not for that, it is first of all because I am anxious to feel in accord with you that I am impatient to know what you think about all this. Tell me also about the conversation you probably had (I saw him in Princeton before his trip) with Father Lynch, who is such a dear soul and who suffers greatly from the New York situation.[3]

We share with all our heart in your joy for the happy birth of baby Caroline. Nancy is now back in her home, we hope to see her and Percy soon, we love them.

Raissa thanks you for your letter. She is delighted that the translation will appear with the original text and with Mr. Matthews' [sic] Note.

I was at hard labor for two months with writing on Dante because of you and Francis. Now I see that this conclusion was quite necessary for my book.

We miss you both. Our love to Caroline and you.

As ever yours
Jacques

I have liked very much your article on Pieper in the N.Y.T. Literary Supplement.[4]

I would like to quote your lecture on Poe and the power of words. Do you intend to publish it in a review or in a book? What reference can I give?

1. Frederick Morgan, a poet and the editor of the *Hudson Review*, was one of several Catholic laymen involved in the formation of an organization called the Committee of Catholics for Cultural Action in 1951. Maritain's letter to Morgan is printed in Appendix A.

2. One of a trilogy of movies by Roberto Rossellini entitled *Ways of Love, The Miracle* was publicly condemned by Francis Cardinal Spellman. Tate wrote a letter to the New York *Times* in which he hotly contested the cardinal's statements. There apparently was some question of legal intervention by the Committee of Catholics for Cultural Action. See the Introduction.

3. William Lynch (1908–87) was a Jesuit priest and well-known teacher and writer. He wrote *Christ and Apollo* (New York, 1960).

4. Josef Pieper (1904—) is a German-born philosopher who has taught and written in the United States since World War II. His works seek to define Western man in terms of Aquinas and Plato.

30

ALLEN TATE TO JACQUES MARITAIN

1801 University Avenue, S.E.
Minneapolis 14, Minnesota
March 2, 1952

My dear Jacques:

Your fine letter to Fred Morgan will greatly strengthen the prudence of the New York group, as it encourages me to believe that what I had written to Robert Fitzgerald, just before your letter arrived, is sound and prudent.[1] As a matter of fact, your letter arrived ten minutes after I had finished my letter to Robert: Father Lynch thought that the "timing" was nothing less than Providential, for had I received your letter first, I should not have been able to deny an imputation of influence. In entirely different language, we had arrived at the same position. I enclose a copy of my letter to Robert.[2]

I had previously, on Wednesday February 27, telegraphed Robert to hold up any action by the group; he had replied on the 28th that no action would be taken until they received further word from me. I am convinced that our letters will persuade the group that the Brief, in the case of The Miracle, should not be filed. —Father Lynch stayed with us four days, during the course of which he completely convinced me that Cardinal Spellman represents, with all his crudity and violence of feeling, an "existential situation" in the Church which it would be folly for us to ignore: he would not be able to judge our actions impartially, but would simply classify us as in opposition to the Church because we are opposing him; and many Catholics of good will, as well as many non-Catholics of ill-will, would believe him.

My opinion from the beginning of my discussions with Morgan and Fitzgerald was that we should form a Catholic literary academy, not a group for political action. The general aims of such an "academy" I have tried to phrase briefly in the last paragraph of my letter to Fitzgerald. That letter in my opinion is a return to my original views; for I have long opposed, publicly and privately, the overt action of American men of letters in immediate political issues; and I see no reason to change my mind now that I am a Catholic. Since the early 1930's American men of letters, Catholic and non-Catholic, have frittered away the advantages of a generally traditional position in a series of skirmishes fought on the ground, and with the weapons, of the "liberal" opposition. Similarly, at the present time, Catholic writers are likely to meet the same frustration *vis-à-vis* the uninformed Philistinism in the Church. I agree with you that the only way to make works of imagination and sensibility a part of Catholic life is to produce enough of them, of sufficient power and distinction, [to] affect the education of the Catholic community as a whole, clergy as well as laity. This is a platitude in the history of literature which we should be very imprudent to neglect.

I had decided, when it became plain that my views, expressed last year, on the aims of a Catholic group, had been superseded, that it would be ungenerous not to go along into the new position; but I was not happy about it. I am grateful to Father Lynch for his far-sighted analysis of the difficulties that we were about to get into: his representations have guided me back to my better judgment. After four days of constant talk with him I am convinced that he is one of the greatest living Churchmen. And his aims are ours. At those points at which we might embarrass his program, we should also frustrate our own.

In this difficult period how I have longed to walk down Nassau Street to Linden Lane! But I must be content with the letters that you can find the time to write. At your leisure I hope you will give me your advice about the desirability of a Catholic *academy*. I cling to that word for two reasons; first, it connotes an exclusion of merely political emphasis; and, secondly, it places a positive emphasis upon intellectual standards. Could we form such an association, Father Lynch assures me that we should quickly get the strong support of the clergy.

I am delighted that you and Raïssa are pleased at the prospect of your translation of my Ode appearing in The Sewanee Review. Mr. Mathews will shortly communicate with you.

If Francis and I led you to write your Dante chapter, we may thank God that He made us his instruments. I am very eager to see the essay. I am much complimented that you wish to quote from my "Poe and the Power of Words." The copy you have is now out of date—not in the opinions, but in the style: I have completely rewritten it. But if you will refer me to the passage that you wish to quote, I will send you the corrected version. The essay will appear in the summer 1952 issue of The Kenyon Review, to follow the publication of the Dante in the spring issue.

The very presence of the Maritain family in Princeton is a source of strength to our children, and we thank God for you. And we pray that He will so dispose all our affairs as to bring us together soon. We send our love to you all.

Affectionately yours,
Allen

1. Robert S. Fitzgerald (1910–85) was a professor of rhetoric at Harvard and an award-winning translator of Homer's *Odyssey* and Virgil's *Aeneid*. He apparently was also a member of the Committee of Catholics for Cultural Action.

2. The letter is printed in Appendix A.

---------- 31 ----------

JACQUES MARITAIN TO ALLEN TATE

[*postcard*]

April 6, 1952

Julian Green's address is: 52bis rue de Varenne, Paris 7e (Telephone: Littré 48-55).

Dear Allen, what splendid news, you are to go to France and we shall see you on May 11!

I think, as you do, that it would be a very good idea to publish the translation of the Ode in a French review. I plan to send it to the Mercure de France, unless you prefer another magazine. A bientôt! Love to you and Caroline

Jacques

---------- 32 ----------

ALLEN TATE TO JACQUES AND RAÏSSA MARITAIN

465 Nassau Street
Princeton
August 4, 1952

Dear Raïssa and Jacques:

We have missed you here this summer. We arrived after many complicated trips, on July 5, and in spite of the brutal heat we have greatly enjoyed the children and the few old friends who are sticking it out through the summer.

I am sending you tear sheets from The Sewanee Review of your magnificent translation of my Ode. Nothing could diminish my pleasure in it. I am however very much annoyed at the editor, who didn't take the trouble to get the right version of the *English* text, so that in many places your translation looks like a mis-translation or at best like a liberty with the text. My *Poems: 1922–1947* is acknowledged as the source, but evidently the editor took the version nearest at hand, perhaps from some old anthology laying [*sic*] on a convenient shelf. I have written a vigorous protest. The Sewanee Review owes you an apology.

The Paris conference is now so far in the past that I shall say of it only that it was not a success.[1] I did enjoy being there, particularly meeting John Thompson and going to see him at Eau Vive.[2] But he has doubtless told you about this. I am coming over again this month, and expect to arrive in Paris on August 21 or 22. This time I am headed for a UNESCO conference on the arts in Venice, September 22–28. The State Department, after inviting me, pointed out the difficulty of appropriating money for a *brief* trip (it is always better to spend more money than less); so I shall get a whole month in Europe in exchange for one speech in Venice. I cannot complain about this. I am to confer with cultural relations officers in Paris, Brussels and Rome before I go to Venice. I do hope that I shall see you in Paris the ten days I am there (Aug. 21–31). I shall probably stop at the Hotel Baltimore (Avenue Kléber), but I can be reached at either the American Embassy or UNESCO. I shall of course communicate at once with John Thompson. I do not like UNESCO, but I decided to go to Venice not only for the pleasure I expect to have (and I don't for a moment discount this motive) but also because of something John Thompson told me. Apparently UNESCO is dominated by atheists, and I hoped that one more person, or perhaps just one person, in Venice who could be said to represent a religious attitude might do a little good.

Caroline will stay on here till September 1, then go on a visit to Missouri, arriving in Minneapolis at about the time I do—September 30.

We send you both our fondest love, and much affection to Vera who we are glad to know can be in France without anxiety. I shall hope to hear from you before I leave or find a message from you when I arrive in Paris.

Affectionately yours,
Allen

1. Tate was a delegate to the Congress for Cultural Freedom in Paris in May, 1952.

2. John Anderson Thompson (1918—) is a literary scholar who wrote *Historical Guide to English Prosody* (1963) and was a regular contributor to the *Kenyon Review* and the *Hudson Review* during this era.

—————————— 33 ——————————

JACQUES MARITAIN TO ALLEN TATE

Paris
August 10, 1952

My very dear Allen:

I am just dropping you a line to give you our address in Paris:

Hôtel St. James
211 rue Saint-Honoré
Paris, 1ᵉʳ

Telephone: Opéra 02-30.

We are elated by this new trip to Paris, and delighted to see you soon. Thank you for your fine letter and for your protest to the Sewanee Review about their blunder.

A bientôt! Our love to Caroline and you, Nancy and Percy.

As ever yours
Jacques

—————————— 34 ——————————

JACQUES MARITAIN TO ALLEN TATE
Monday morning
August 24, 1952

My very dear Allen:

I wrote to the Reverend Heston (by mail) and to my friend Mgr. Fontenelle (I enclose the letter).[1] Do not fail to pay a visit to him, he is a dear friend of ours, and is very influential. His address: Mgr. R. Fontenelle, Canonica di San Pietro, Città del Vaticano.

Some other addresses:[2]

Signorina Matilda Mazzolani, via Panisperna 207 (Telephone: 46.436) She was my secretary, she is extremely kind and helpful,—speaks English.

They are probably absent   ⎧ Révérend Père Delos, Canonist Counsellor,
now, I hope they will   ← ⎨
return in September.   ⎩ Révérend Père Darsy, Cultural Attaché,

both at the French Embassy to the Holy See, 23 via Piave, Roma. Father

Darsy is an extremely good archeologist, the best possible guide in Rome. (Directed the restauration [*sic*] of Santa Sabina).

Révérend Père Paul Philippe, Collegio Angelico, 1, Salita del Grillo, Roma. A great authority in spiritual matters and a lover of your country. (Is now in America, will be back in Rome soon).

My marvelous friend Father Giovanni de Menasce (the cousin of Father Pierre de Menasce). Also a lover of America. 29 via Marianna Dionigi, Roma.

Both speak English.

You may also visit another friend, Mgr. André Baron, Rector of San Luigi dei Francesi, Via Giovanna d'Arco, 5, Roma.

All of them can assist you, one way or other.

I forgot to tell you that there are two kinds of audiences with the Pope: either *private* audience alone with him in his study, or *special* audience, which lasts only five minutes, sometimes with a few other people. It is a private audience that I wish for you, though it is more difficult to obtain.

On the other hand, do not forget to ask an audience with Mgr. Montini (I wrote about that to Mgr. Fontenelle;—to the Rev. Heston I spoke only of the audience with the Pope).[3]

It was a profound joy for all three of us to see you Friday. We pray the good Angels to bless your trip and pilgrimage! Pray for us. To you our love

Jacques

1. The Reverend Edward L. Heston (1908–73) was an American priest who held various positions at the Vatican. The letter to Mgr. Fontenelle is printed in Appendix A.
2. In preparation for Tate's visit to Venice.
3. The future pope Paul VI, Giovanni Montini was a friend of Maritain's during the latter's tenure as French ambassador to the Vatican and a student of Maritain's writings.

35

JACQUES MARITAIN TO ALLEN TATE

26 Linden Lane
Princeton, N.J.
November 27, 1952

Dear Allen:

Your poem has marvellous rhythm and plenitude and musicality and we admire it deeply. We are eager to know the entire poem.[1]

What bad luck! Tuesday, December 2 I must fly to San Francisco, and shall be back Saturday night, the sixth. Please stay in Princeton one day more! It was a misfortune to miss you in October. I would be inconsolable if I could not see you Sunday the 7th.

Pardon me for writing in haste. Raissa is not too well for the time being. A bientôt, dear Allen. Pray for us. Our deep love to Caroline and you. Nous vous embrassons

Jacques

1. Veronica Makowsky, in *Caroline Gordon: A Biography* (New York, 1989), 198, says that Tate's last productive period as a poet was the early 1950s, when he wrote "The Maimed Man," "The Swimmers," and "The Buried Lake." Maritain must have been referring to one of these poems.

36

JACQUES MARITAIN TO ALLEN TATE AND CAROLINE GORDON

Princeton, N.J.
January 26, 1954

Dearest Allen and Caroline,

We think of you with love and nostalgia. We hope you are happy in Rome. Pray St. Benoît Labre for me at Santa Maria dei Monti. To you both our fervent wishes and deep affection.

Your
Jacques

37

JACQUES MARITAIN TO CAROLINE GORDON

Princeton
May 5, 1954

Dear Caroline,

A thousand thanks for your letter and the Review. I read your story about Gide and his wife with immense pleasure, a story which is written with such power of emotion, human compassion and generosity.[1] (In actual fact, when she married him she knew nothing, I think you changed that purposedly). Our dearest love to you and Allen and Nancy and Percy. You are always in the hearts of Raïssa, Vera, and

Jacques

I am beginning to get up for a few moments.[2]

Is your big undescript future Victorian house not too far from Linden Lane?

1. The story, entitled "Emmanuele! Emmanuele!," is found in Caroline Gordon, *"Old Red" and Other Stories* (New York, 1963), 26–68. It was first published in the *Sewanee Review*, LXII (1954), 181–222.

2. See Appendix A for a letter from Maritain's secretary, Cornelia Borgerhoff, informing the Tates of Maritain's heart attack in March of 1954.

38

CAROLINE GORDON TO JACQUES MARITAIN

465 Nassau Street
Princeton, New Jersey
May 7, 1954

Dear Jacques:

Allen keeps asking for news of you and it is hard for him to understand why I don't call oftener at 16 Linden Lane to get it. (He has never been a grandmother!) I am so glad to have some report on your health for him in your own words, though half-angry with you for spending any effort on acknowledging my story.

At the same time, I must confess that I do not think I have ever received praise that I valued more. Something strange has happened to the novel in the last half century. There are not many people who realize that it is or should be a work of art. I verily believe that Tom Eliot is among these people or he would not have uttered his pronouncement to the effect that it was dead as an art form, when it is just getting under weigh [*sic*].

I am pleased on two counts to have you like "Emmanuele." Of course Gide did most of the work for me. The details were all ready to hand in his letters, his memoirs and that memoir Roger Martin du Gard wrote.[1] But it is good to know that you of all people found my story a true fiction.

I am sending you another piece of "light reading" which you are not, on any account, to bother to acknowledge.[2] (I am quite serious about this.) When I give this piece as a lecture I try to disarm criticism from the Logical Positivists with which every campus swarms by pointing out that though my progress is, logically, a little like that of Eliza in "Uncle Tom's Cabin," when she crossed the Ohio river by leaping from one ice-cake to another (I, perforce, leap from intuition to intuition!) I have a friend on the bank who is kind enough to keep a bon-fire going to light my perilous path. As I wrote you recently there are four passages in *Art and Scholasticism*, on which I base my piece, that have been of more practical help to me than anything I have ever read.[3] I don't even except *The Poetics*.

Nancy is enormously improved, almost herself again. Her condition has been somewhat complicated, I suspect, by the fact that Percy is a psychiatrist. What in my day would have been a threatened nervous breakdown, occasioned partly by excessive physical fatigue and worry (they must owe everybody in town!) becomes these days an "episode." Percy is about to start private practise. He has done marvellously at the Institute in Philadelphia. Every time I see him I am impressed by how much he has matured since we last met. I have a notion that in time he will slip under the mantle of Jung—his mind seems to incline that way. At present he is wrestling with Father Sigmund. Since, as Allen observes in his "Mediterranean," "We have cracked the hemispheres with careless hands" there seems nothing for young men to do except to dive into the abyss caused by the crack (that old Cartesian crack about which you have written so eloquently.)[4] Percy is right out in front on our new frontier!

I have asked Allen to get us news of Fr. de Menasce but haven't had time to hear from him about that yet. He says he is trying to write a review of your book for *Encounter*.[5] I think that he must be in fine fettle to attempt such a task. As you know, he is enormously impressed by it.

Nancy, Percy and I spent last Sunday cleaning and frantically polishing up this dilapidated little house in the hopes of snaring a purchaser. The first person who saw it bought it—for twenty five thousand dollars, which was more than the banks thought we'd get out of it. We are buying the Hodge Road place for twenty three thousand. At the moment I am regarded as a financial genius by the family. But I am very poor at that sort of thing and it has been a great strain. We hope to move into the new place May fifteenth. It is 54 Hodge Road, just off Library Place. There are three and one half bathrooms and six bedrooms and room enough for Allen and me to stay when we come to Princeton instead of having to rent a place. We are all blissful at the prospect. Allen has been heroic, giving his consent for me to go ahead with all sort of manoeuvres. I may go back to Italy after we get the children established in the new house or he may come over here. If he does he forfeits about two thousand dollars, since he's paid in *lire*. On the other hand, he longs for a cubicle in the Princeton Library. He has never been able to work in a foreign country and feels about Italy the way Hawthorne did: "I fear that this Italian air does not favour close toil."

This long note is written in lieu of a visit, since it can be written while I baby sit. Raissa will not deliver it to you, I know, if you have too much other correspondence to deal with, and I really mean it about not acknowledging the piece in the *Sewanee*.

Our love to all three of you. We are so happy that you are improving,

Caroline

Allen is representing the United States at Mayor La Pira's Christian Congress in Florence. His speech will be largely his comments on your new book: "It will be just the right thing, for Jacques' theory of art boils down to the doctrine that Culture cannot survive without Revelation."

1. Roger Martin du Gard (1881–1958) was a French novelist and contemporary of André Gide. His eight-part *Les Thibault* (Paris, 1922–40) won him the Nobel Prize in 1937.

2. Caroline Gordon, "Some Readings and Misreadings," *Sewanee Review*, LXI (1953), 384–407.

3. Jacques Maritain, *Art & Scholasticism, with Other Essays,* trans. J. F. Scanlan (New York, 1930).

4. Allen Tate, *"The Mediterranean" & Other Poems* (New York, 1936).

5. Gordon is referring to Maritain's definitive book on aesthetics, *Creative Intuition in Art and Poetry,* which includes "Texts Without Comment," passages from some of his favorite writers in illustration of his views. Tate's poetry figures prominently in "Texts."

39

JACQUES MARITAIN TO CAROLINE GORDON

Princeton
June 6, 1954

Dear Caroline:

I suppose that all the dear family is now gathered in the huge house of Hodge Road. Did you finish establishing them? Can you have some rest now? I am not yet very good for conversation but I hope that I shall shortly be able to ask you to come home. Don't tell me that you plan to return now to Italy! I trust that Allen is to come over here—I am delighted that he was in Florence and met the saintly La Pira,—and extremely proud that in his speech he had comments on my book.

By the two Tates I am spoiled indeed. What a good fortune for a philosopher to have his thoughts elucidated and illustrated in real life as you did with these passages from Art and Scholasticism in your article on the novel in the Sewanee Review! All that you say about the Christian Scheme of Redemption in great modern novelists is extraordinarily true. I like very much your remarks on Henry James and Joyce in particular.

My friend John Nef told me he sent a copy of his wife's book to Allen and hopes eagerly that Allen will write a recension.[1] I beg him to do so if he likes the book,—I shall tell you how important it is for John, I mean for his heart and very life. Elinor was a great, strange and generous personality. We had great affection for her. She had acute insight, and was passionate to understand people.

A bientôt, dear Caroline. Our love to you and Nancy and Percy. As ever yours

Jacques

1. John U. Nef (1899–1988) was an author and professor of economic history. He founded the Committee on Social Thought, an elite interdisciplinary graduate program at the University of Chicago, where he was also a collaborator in the Great Books program. The book referred to is Elinor Castle Nef's *Letters and Notes*, ed. John U. Nef (Los Angeles, 1953).

40

CAROLINE GORDON AND ALLEN TATE TO JACQUES AND RAÏSSA MARITAIN

[*Christmas card*]

Minneapolis
December 14, 1954[1]

Dearest Maritains,

We miss you daily and you are in our daily prayers. We hear that Jacques is doing well, and we are thankful. We are comfortably settled for the winter and are at work. Our love to all three of you.

Allen

Jacques: Allen sat up half last night, reading your new book.[2] He's very excited about it and says it is going to be of great help to him. We miss you all very much, and look forward to seeing you next summer.

The first snow of the winter has fallen. It will be on the ground till next March! We have rented a house on the banks of the Mississippi river—from a professor of Comparative Religions, who is off to Calcutta. The place is full of bronze Dancing Shivas—I have to sprinkle a little Holy Water around every now and then, to keep things in order. We have a very handsome modern church almost in our back yard, Mother Cabrini. The ribs of the nave are all exposed and are shaped like the hull of a Viking ship. It's really terrific, so terrific that it may make a daily communicant of me.

Dearest love to all three of you. Take good care of yourselves,

as ever,
Caroline

1. City and date come from the postmark on the envelope.
2. *Creative Intuition in Art and Poetry.*

41

RAÏSSA MARITAIN TO ALLEN TATE

Princeton
2 February 1955

Dear Allen,

Your letter touches and reassures me. I am much happier to know that my book stayed in Princeton in the confusion of the departure than to imagine that it is in Minneapolis and that you don't like it.[1] I was afraid of you because you are a great and severe critic as well as a great and demanding poet. This is to tell you how happy I am that you said you do like my poetry. I shall await patiently the time when it will be possible for you to recover my book in Princeton. If we aren't then in France, Jacques would gladly read some of my poems to you. He reads them marvelously well, with simplicity and such a subtle sense of their rhythm. I myself am absolutely incapable of reading them, because I hear them in my own silence. I suppose that is how a musician hears within himself what he composes.

We miss you and Caroline. Our health is better. We think of you both with all our hearts. Pray for us.

With my love, as ever
Raïssa

1. Raïssa Maritain, *Au creux du rocher* (Paris, 1954), her newly published collection of poems.

42

JACQUES MARITAIN TO CAROLINE GORDON

26 Linden Lane
Princeton, N.J.
March 28, 1956

Dear Caroline:

I just finished your book, few books moved me so deeply: perhaps because I felt everywhere the vivid presence of your heart.[1] This book is full of poetry,—implacable and loving, et d'un dessin admirablement sûr.[2] Not to speak of masterly à-côtés,[3] like that discourse of the enseminator which I enjoy so much. The fact of your characters being haunted by real figures very close to us, Hart Crane, Dorothy Day, Peter Maurin (and probably many others whom I did not recognize) gives them a very strange dimension and renders them curiously familiar to us.[4] This has nothing to do with the *roman à clé*, it is rather a use of overtones which seems to me very new and bold, and very successful. But the great thing is the sense of the lovingkindness of Our Lord which permeates the entire book.[5] The epigraph makes me awfully proud,—I did not remember having uttered so profound a sentence, and I suspect that you have made it better than the original.

We miss you and Allen. When shall we see you? We are having a little relief now, after ceaseless health troubles. So tired that we are obliged to give up our trip to France,—will go to East Hampton in the summer.

Pray for us. Our fervent wishes and dearest love to you both

Jacques

Raïssa is eager to read *The Malefactors*. But I detained the book until now.

1. Maritain refers to Gordon's novel *The Malefactors* (New York, 1956), which carries a quotation from his book *The Frontiers of Poetry* as its epigraph: "It is for Adam to interpret the voices that Eve hears."

2. "And of an admirably firm design."

3. "Asides."

4. Hart Crane (1899–1932), an American poet, had a sometimes stormy relationship with the Tates and even spent the winter of 1925–26 under their roof in a rented pre-Revolutionary War farmhouse in upstate New York. Peter Maurin (1877–1949) was co-founder, with Dorothy Day, of the Catholic Worker movement in the 1930s. Day described him as "a genius, a saint, an agitator, a writer, a lecturer, a poor man, and a shabby tramp, all in one" (William B. Miller, *Dorothy Day: A Biography* [San Francisco, 1982], 228). In Ann Waldron's *Close Connections: Caroline Gordon and the Southern Renaissance* (New York, 1987), 297, we learn that Tate once said Day was the most impressive person he had ever met. According to Waldron, Day, Gordon, and Tate conceived a plan for a new writers' conference in which daily liturgical life would be fully integrated. The students would pay no tuition and eat food grown on Maryfarm, the site of the conference. "And when a student would bring her a manuscript and ask her what was wrong with it, Caroline said the answer might be, 'What's wrong with you?' " (297).

5. "The lovingkindness of our Lord" is Gordon's translation of Maritain's original, which is in Greek (Titus 3:4).

43

CAROLINE GORDON TO JACQUES MARITAIN

April 19, 1956
1339 Ohio Street
Lawrence, Kansas

Dear Jacques:

I am, indeed, sorry to hear that you and the ladies will not go to France this summer. I know that you must all need the refreshment. I am not consoled even by the reflection that your loss may be our gain; we may catch a glimpse of you between all our various peregrinations. We, by the way, will be more your neighbours from now on. We have taken one of Anne Fremantle's little houses at 154 Mercer Street and from now on expect to spend most of each summer there.[1] Allen, of course, will have to dash here and there, lecturing, but I am willing to endure Princeton heat for the sake of a chance to do a little gardening.

It was so good of you to write me about my book. I cannot tell you how happy your letter made me. Allen says "If you write a book which is an innovation both in subject matter and form you must expect to be attacked," and I did expect—not to be attacked so viciously, but ignored, as usual. To have the book really read, as you have read it, is a wonderful thing. Since it is a sort of attempt to embody what you say about Adam and Eve I am even more delighted to find that it meets with your approval.[2]

The epigraph, whether or not you remember uttering it, is, indeed, profound. I, being a novelist, concern myself chiefly with its fleshly references. Fr. Simon, who, in "The Commonweal," wrote the only review of "The Malefactors" which I have found worth reading, takes your saying on a higher—or deeper level. I'll quote it since you may not have seen that issue of the magazine:

> This text, taken from Maritain's essay, 'The Frontiers of Poetry,' is to be understood as specifying the relationship between the practical or critical intelligence and poetic intuition—Claudel's *animus* and *anima*. Man's critical intelligence is situated between a lower and higher intuition. These realms on either side of the practical reason can be mistaken for each other. The one has an obscurity 'by excess of opacity;' the other an obscurity by 'excess of transparence.' The poet is nourished by his intuitions, but it is the critical intelligence (Adam) which must decide on the authenticity of what the soul (Eve) experiences.[3]

When I was in Rome a few years ago I used often to see Chirico walking about the Piazza da Spagna, with his coat-collar turned up as if against some invisible and infernal blast, and would think of what you say in "Creative Intuition" about the artist's listening to his "automatic unconscious" and mistaking what he hears for something going on in Plato's Cave.[4] You were talking about painting but what you say is very relevant to the novel, and has been of great help to me.

I am therefore enormously pleased by your discernments and comments on the techniques used in my book. I believe it is the first time that what James called his "great compositional law" of "the angle of vision" or "central consciousness" has been used consistently and exhaustively. But I believe, too, that, as you have divined, I have succeeded in adding another dimension in using the Jungian "underground" as a setting for action, not only throughout the book, but in the *dénouement*, when Horne Watts sends Claiborne to see Catherine Pollard.

Catherine Pollard, Horne Watts, Joseph Tardieu and Quintus Claiborne are in there, of course, because three of them are dead and one of them is a saint and they therefore *can* furnish another plane of action. In the light of the technical uses to which these identifiable persons have been put it has been amusing—and annoying—to have people speculating on "who" they are—and to have my novel compared to Mary McCarthy's latest "strip-tease," in which every character is identifiable in the vulgar sense.[5]

As for Catherine Pollard, Denver Lindley sent a copy of "The Malefactors" to Dorothy Day, asking her to help introduce it into Catholic circles.[6] She replied that if she had her way she would burn every copy! Poor Denver had taken it for granted that I would have shown her the manuscript, since the book was dedicated to her. But some still, small voice had warned me not to. Malcolm Cowley once observed that "Writing is one of the gifts the Holy Ghost hasn't given Dorothy."[7] I'd add reading. I was distressed a bit—chiefly for poor Denver's sake; he had to rip out the dedication and "tip in" a page substituting "alchemical experiments" for "Black masses." [B]ut he had lunch with Dorothy, as the result of all the commotion, and reported that he found her even more impressive than I had made her out, and that was very worth while for him, as I think he is drawing near the Church.

Flannery O'Connor, who, to my mind, is the most gifted of the younger fiction writers, comforted me by recalling that when your godfather first saw Roua[u]lt's paintings he went all over Paris, calling out loudly for "a true Catholic painter."[8] I was flattered by the comparison, but even more flattered—and cheered—by your letter. It is a wonderful thing for a novelist to be able to count you and Raïssa among her readers. I am almost ashamed when I think of really great novelists who never had such luck.

Allen and I look forward to seeing you all soon. I am so glad that the illnesses have let up. I have heard about them from various sources and have felt that the Maritains were really getting more than their share. I do so hope it will be a good spring. Until we see you again, our love for all three of you,

Caroline

A letter just came from Denver, saying he had got permission to quote from your letter which, in my pride and vanity, I sent him. Again, thanks!

1. Anne Fremantle (1910—), a British subject born in France and a naturalized American citizen, was converted to Catholicism in 1943. She was an editor, a broadcaster, and a professor at Fordham University from 1948 to 1961.

2. See note 1 of No. 42.

3. The Reverend John W. Simon, Review of Caroline Gordon's *The Malefactors*, in *Commonweal*, April 13, 1956, pp. 54–56.

4. Giorgio de Chirico (1888–1978) was an Italian painter and precursor of surrealism. His radically innovative style was called "metaphysical painting." Maritain wrote of him in *Creative Intuition in Art and Poetry*.

5. This most likely would have been McCarthy's *A Charmed Life* (New York, 1955).

6. Denver Lindley (1904–82) was an editor and translator of Thomas Mann, Erich Maria Remarque, and André Maurois.

7. Malcolm Cowley (1898–1989) was a film critic for the New York *Times* and a longtime friend of Gordon and Tate.

8. Maritain's godfather was Léon Bloy (1846–1917), a fiery French polemicist and mystic who had a decisive role in the conversion of the Maritains. The Maritains knew the French painter Georges Rouault (1871–1958) well during their residence in Versailles just before World War I.

44

JACQUES MARITAIN TO CAROLINE GORDON

Box 1043
East Hampton, N.Y.
September 8, 1956

Dear Caroline:

Your lovely letter was a boon. We are delighted that you have become now Princetonian landowners, and that this old house is so perfectly fitting your bents, purposes, hobbies, principles and prejudices. We are returning to Princeton in Mid-September and hope very much to see you there. Vacation in East Hampton began with new anxieties about Vera's health, which are over now. Vera is still weak, but doing well. Raissa and I are, so to speak, recovering with her, and all three of us begin to take breath. May the coming year be less rude than the past one!

Thank you ever so much for all that you tell me about the *Malefactors*. The only ghost I did not recognize was Chirico (I never met him, only saw him from afar, painting in the gardens of Villa Medici one of the *pompier* things he is now doing). Your comparison with the gods and goddesses in Homer is quite illuminating.

Did you know that Julian Green published (about at the same time) a novel in French: *Le Malfaiteur* (on an entirely different subject)?

What you tell me about *Art and Scholasticism* gives me great joy— that so unfrequent joy for a philosopher in realizing that his thought has been understood *in depth*,—this makes the work, if I dare say, somewhat acceptable to the Angels. About the Novel there are some remarks in the last chapter of *Creative Intuition* about which I would like very much to have your impression, if you have the time of looking at them one day.

Viking had a splendid idea in asking you *How to Read a Novel*.[1] That's a passionately interesting subject, for the instruction of the common reader and that of the critic, both of them, as a rule, are equally dull though in opposite directions.

Jack Wheelock is absent for the moment.[2] He rented his house to some twenty male Carmelites who made it into a convent, I was told that the Master of Novices was lost in the woods one day.

I hope that Allen enjoyed his foreign seminar.

Our love to you both. A bientôt!

As ever yours,
Jacques

1. Caroline Gordon, *How to Read a Novel* (New York, 1957).
2. John Hall Wheelock (1886–1978) was a longtime editor for Scribner's and a poet of some distinction. He was also instrumental in introducing such poets as James Dickey, Louis Simpson, and Joseph Langland.

45

JACQUES MARITAIN TO CAROLINE GORDON

26 Linden Lane
Princeton, N.J.
October 3, 1956

Dear Caroline:

What you tell me about Allen makes us quite distressed.[1] I do not believe it would be a good idea to try to see him,—he obviously does not wish it. Raïssa and I are writing a few lines to him, telling him of our love.

We shall see you as soon as I am back from Notre Dame. Our hearts are deeply with you, in your sorrow and your prayers.

To you our dearest love

Jacques

P.S. You told me that Allen lives now at the Princeton Club. But there is no Princeton Club? I telephoned to Nassau Club and to Princeton Inn, he is not there. Please send me his complete address as soon as possible, dear Caroline, so that I can send our letter to him.

And give me also your telephone number!

1. Gordon and Tate were in the process of their definitive separation, having already been divorced once and remarried. Their final divorce was legally declared in 1959.

46

JACQUES AND RAÏSSA MARITAIN TO ALLEN TATE

26 Linden Lane
Princeton, N.J.
October 3, 1956

Dear Allen,

I was just told that you are leaving for India soon. How much I regret not to be able to see you before! I myself am leaving for Notre Dame University. These few lines bring all our wishes and greetings to you. We think of you with deep affection, we beg the holy Angels to accompany you and help you, and to be with you everywhere. Who can cherish poets and poetry more than they do? I wish you may know how dear you are to our hearts, how close we are to you. Pray for us as we pray for you.

To you my love
Jacques
and mine
Raïssa

47

ALLEN TATE TO JACQUES MARITAIN

The Princeton Club
of New York
October 8, 1956

Dear Jacques,

Your letter was awaiting me when I arrived here yesterday and I am deeply moved that you and Raïssa were thinking of me on the eve of my trip to India. I leave today at seven on Air France. I shall stop in Paris for a day, and Rome for two days; and then on to New Delhi.

Not to have seen you during the summer was a privation, but I knew that Vera's illness and convalescence came before all else. I pray that she is fully recovered. I shall count on seeing you all in December.

Caroline has told you that we may live apart in the future. At present I do not see how otherwise the love and compassion of thirty-two years, which underlie our marriage, can prevail in our hearts. It is in God's hands, and we shall wait.

I trust that your own health is better and that your time at Notre Dame will not be too strenuous. Please pray for me and for Caroline. My love to you all,

Allen

48

CAROLINE GORDON TO JACQUES MARITAIN

Wednesday, 18 oct. 56[1]

Dear Jacques:

I'll be delighted to come to see you all on October twenty second.

But don't have me on your mind! I told you about Allen's situation in the faint hope that he might see you before he left. Of course that was impossible and I'm sorry I caught you just when you were so occupied with your lecture—but when is a writer ever not occupied?

Allen *is* in a bad way, but then, as I said, he is subject to these seizures, during which his whole personality seems to undergo a great change, every four or five years. It is, I suspect, a trouble to which poets have always been particularly prone. And no doubt it is intimately connected with his genius. If he is in a bad way now I am confident that he will soon be in a much better way. Already I see signs of that. (His seizures follow an easily identifiable pattern.)

We are all prone to psychologize every human situation these days. I find myself tempted to view Allen's situation mythologically, however. It seems to me that both in private and public life that [*sic*] he over and over enacts the role of Adonis. This assigns me the uncongenial *role* of the Queen and Huntress (more than life-size, alas,) attended by fanged, wild beasts! (It is unfortunate for me that the heraldic emblem of my family is the wild boar!)

I am convinced that the sacrifices which Adonis and Tammuz and all those old world demi-gods and heroes made were acceptable to God— but that was before Christ came "to make all things new." And now they avail "no more than the blood of bullocks." Allen had portrayed over and over and most brilliantly the plight of the old-world hero sacrificed to "The Great Mother." But he has undertaken a new song: a long poem in honour of Our Lady. He may have to become a new man in order to write it.

I sound awfully smug, as if everything were wrong with him and nothing wrong with me. But every day I am more and more aware of the part my own weaknesses and faults have played in our troubles. I make scenes and reproach him for things he has done—and I must say he does dreadful things! Fr. Lynch says that Allen has "one of the most Catholic minds in America," and he probably has, but neither of us has Catholic habits and neither of us is a good Christian.

This psychological-mythological double talk is boring, I know, but I resort to it as a kind of short-hand—to get all this out of the way so that we may talk of other matters when we meet. And the details of our troubles are even more boring![2] And this letter requires no answer—I know how pressed for time you are.

I assume that Vera continues to improve. I was so happy to see her looking so much herself the other day! Love for you all,

Caroline

I have begun driving the car again and am now licensed to do so by the State of New Jersey, a fact which rouses wild pride in this bosom. Tell the ladies of your household that if they wish to entrust me with their shopping lists at the A. and P. I'll be delighted to buy the groceries and deliver them to 26 Linden Lane. I am only two blocks from the Shopping Centre and the parking there is delightful.

1. The date was written in by hand, apparently by Maritain.
2. This sentence was handwritten at the bottom of the typed letter with an arrow leading into the text.

─────────────────── 49 ───────────────────

JACQUES MARITAIN TO CAROLINE GORDON

Princeton, N.J.
November 13, 1956

Dear Caroline,

I am back from Chicago. Is it possible for you to come and see us Saturday (Nov. 17) at 5:30? I hope that at last we can speak with you at leisure, and speak of all that is dear to our hearts!

With all our love,
As ever yours,
Jacques

─────────────────── 50 ───────────────────

JACQUES MARITAIN TO ALLEN TATE

26 Linden Lane
Princeton, N.J.
January 19, 1957

Dear Allen:

I just heard about your Bollingen prize. That's a great joy for all three of us. We send you our warmest and most affectionate congratulations. This prize is but a sign. I wish you might realize how deeply the American spirit and all lovers of poetry are indebted to you.

It was good to see you here. All that you told me I keep in my heart. Raissa and I are thinking of you with profound love.

Pray for us.

As ever yours,
Jacques

ALLEN TATE TO JACQUES MARITAIN

University of Minnesota
College of Science, Literature, and
the Arts
Minneapolis 14
February 6, 1957

Dear Jacques,

Your note about the Bollingen Prize was deeply pleasing to me. Yours was the only letter from Princeton. For some reason which I do not yet understand, the award threw me into a depression for several days. I suppose the reason was my failure to accomplish any fundamental work in several years. Hamlet's words echoed in my ear: "How all occasions do inform against me!"

Caroline wrote me recently that she had been to see you all, and had come away much encouraged. I know you have great responsibilities but if you can keep your spiritual eye on her I shall have one more reason to be grateful to you.

For your eye alone: I am going regularly to a Catholic psychotherapist, as the result of Father Lynch's advice given when I saw him in Washington a month ago.

I shall hope to see you and Raïssa and Vera late in March. Meanwhile I hope that Raïssa is well and that Vera continues to improve. I am always thinking of your own health; please safeguard it. Pray for me.

My love to you all,
Allen

JACQUES MARITAIN TO CAROLINE GORDON

Monday February 25

Dear Caroline:

Are you free Wednesday (the day after tomorrow) February 27, and can you come at 5 o clock? I shall be so glad to see you.

If you are teaching in New York Wednesday, could you come Saturday (March 2) at the same time?

Love from all three of us

> As ever yours,
> Jacques

53

JACQUES MARITAIN TO ALLEN TATE

26 Linden Lane
Princeton, N.J.
February 28, 1957

My very dear Allen,

Your dear letter made me happy. I am so glad that you are going regularly to the Catholic psychotherapist recommended by Father Lynch, and that he seems to be really helpful.

Today I am writing in haste apropos of Caroline, with whom I had a long talk yesterday. She is exceedingly sorry about the way in which she spoke to you on the telephone, and she asked me to tell you how repentant she is. The fault, I am sure, lies with that woman, that so-called friend she saw in New York, and with the venom of her gossip.

I hope you will tell Caroline that all that is forgotten. She felt miserable but is much better now, and more hopeful. She is anxious to do all that she can to help; expects you to come to Princeton for the spring vacation. I think that these few days in Princeton will be of very great importance for her and you. As for the three of us, you know how eager we are to see you. A bientôt donc!

Vera is better but still very weak. We three are terribly tired; hoping for the sun. Pray for us, dear Allen.

To you our dearest love

> As ever yours,
> Jacques

54

CAROLINE GORDON TO JACQUES MARITAIN

Thursday
February 28, 1957[1]

Dear Jacques:

The talk I had with you yesterday has done me great good and I hope and pray that it will result in good for Allen—and Nancy, too.

You asked if I had another book in mind to write. I don't, really. I feel just now like a Western Union messenger boy who has been assured that he won't have to go out any more on dark and stormy nights. Still, I *have* got the *title* of a book: *The Air of The Country*. You remember that Pere de Caussade says that if you like the air of the country why not go there?[2] I read the book in translation and this is one phrase which, I think, has not suffered in translation. If I do succeed in writing it I will be following—at a distance—in Raïssa's foot-steps—her book has meant a great deal to me. One of the sorrows of my life is that I can't talk with her more freely, my French being practically non-existent now. I wrote my first novel in Paris—on Allen's Guggenheim fellowship.[3] I knew it was sink or swim for me, as a writer, as I could afford a nurse for Nancy there and I couldn't afford one in this country—so I resolutely turned my back on one language in order to deal with another. Too resolutely, I see now, as I seem to have got a kind of "block" against speaking French. I still marvel at your command of English in *Creative Intuition*!

God bless you all, as He does, and thanks for all you have done for us,

Caroline

1. The date is penciled in, presumably by Maritain.

2. Jean-Pierre de Caussade (1675–1751) was the French Jesuit who wrote the spiritual classic *De l'abandon à la providence divine* (On abandonment to divine providence, *ca.* 1860).

3. Caroline Gordon, *Penhally* (New York, 1931).

55

ALLEN TATE TO JACQUES MARITAIN

University of Minnesota
College of Science, Literature, and
the Arts
Minneapolis 14
March 8, 1957

My dear Jacques,

I have been much affected and reassured by your letter, and also by a letter, a day later, from Caroline. After all these years I ought not to be upset when Caroline is in distress, but rather should meet it with charity and a sense of my responsibility for having largely caused it. I quite realize that my coming to Princeton for the spring vacation will be of great importance to both her and me, and for that reason I have doubted whether this is the time to come: it might invite disaster, so soon after the recent upset, and the results might be irremediable. I am pondering and praying over this, and I shall decide accordingly.

What happened, of course, is that that malicious woman insinuated certain things which are not true, but which released Caroline's memory of injury at my hands more than ten years ago. At such moments her emotions are beyond control. I have not been able to make adequate amends for that old injury. That, briefly, is our trouble, as I see it.

Your letter has been like a beacon in the night—the compassion and charity which do not judge. I am deeply grateful, and send you-all my love.

Allen

56

JACQUES MARITAIN TO ALLEN TATE

26 Linden Lane
Princeton, N.J.
March 21, 1957

My dear Allen,

I was touched to the heart by your letter,—as I was also by my talk with Caroline. So deep a mutual love, and such suffering at the core of it!

I have no doubt that God will help you, make His peace prevail. But I also realize that you are right in pondering and praying over the advisability of your coming to Princeton for the spring vacation.

Whatever decision you will make, it will be made in the light of prayer.

If you thought it is preferable not to come, the question, it seems to me, would be then to reassure Caroline, in making clear to her the reasons for this postponement. I believe that she is anxious, as you are, about the possible dangers involved in your coming now, but that, at the same time, she will be, if you don't come, greatly disappointed and sorry, and in need of being comforted, especially because of those things she said to you on the telephone and which she regrets so much.

Dear Allen, you know with what profound love Raissa and I are thinking of you. Pray for us.

Yours as ever,
Jacques

57

JACQUES MARITAIN TO ALLEN TATE

26 Linden Lane
Princeton, N.J.
March 4, 1958

Dear Allen,

Your letter is a treasure which I cherish and which gives me wonderful encouragement. I wrote this book in fear and trembling (the trembling of love),—what you tell me about it is too generous, to be sure, but reassures me in an invaluable manner.[1] Now I think that I was not too presumptuous in trying to give this kind of testimony,—the last thing I could do, in my old age, to conclude so many years of work in this country, and of love for it. I thank you from the bottom of my heart.

Yes, we shall be in Princeton the last five days of March, and we hope eagerly to see you. Would you be so kind as to telephone to us upon your arrival? (Walnut 4-1616).

We miss you terribly.

I was delighted to know through my good friends the Fathers of Assumption University that you will receive there the Christian Culture Award. I am sure you will like Father Murphy and Father Garvey.

Pray for us, dear Allen.

To you the love of all three of us. A bientôt!

> Je vous embrasse
> Jacques

1. Undoubtedly Jacques Maritain, *Reflections on America* (New York, 1958).

58

CAROLINE GORDON TO JACQUES MARITAIN

> 145 Ewing Street
> Princeton, New Jersey
> March 16, 1960[1]

Dear Jacques:

You again put me deeply in your debt with your new book, *The Responsibility of the Artist.*[2] It is based, I see, on the lectures which I could have heard in 1951—if I had not been too stupid and slothful to get around to hearing them. However, I'm not too sorry about that as I doubt if I could have understood much of them then—and anyhow, it is better to be able to read what you have to say.

Your book comes to me at a good time. A Catholic bureau has asked me to lecture for them and I promptly lifted out of your book the title I needed for a lecture on the art of fiction: "The Key to the Plot."

Many thanks, and many, many thanks, dear Jacques, for all your work. I'm not capable, of course, of understanding a lot, but when I do understand something you say that saying is, for me, more vital and energizing than anything anybody else is saying to me nowadays. . . . I read, off and on, in *Creative Intuition*, and have now, for some years, but this new book has sent me back to thorough re-reading of *Creative Intuition*.

I also found your book on America very enlightening and helpful. I am working—in my fashion—on the same theme. I'm immersed now in a new novel. The section I'm working on is called *A Visit to the Grove*—(of Ashtaroth. They are my own people. I'm sure I have compassion for them but I don't as yet feel quite as kindly to them as you do!)[3]

I think of you and Raïssa so often and of dear Vera, whose life was so beautiful.[4] Francis Fergusson attended her requiem Mass with me and I could see that he was much moved. I suspect that he is very near the Church.

My love to you both,

as ever,
Caroline

When I read what you have to say about art—any of the arts—I am always reminded of what Chekhov said—that if he could only learn to *read talentedly* he would fire quite a cannon ......You are, I believe, the most talented reader I have ever known.

Historical note: My great great great grandfather, "Parson" Douglas, came to the colonies as tutor in the family of the elder James Monroe. His favorite pupil was "Tommy" Jefferson. He used to ask the other students why they couldn't be as clever as "Tommy." Another favorite pupil was Meriwether Lewis, whom he admired for his knowledge of the wilds. When Lewis was fighting in "the Whiskey Rebellion" he found time to identify nineteen varieties of ferns and half a dozen wildflowers that weren't found in Virginia. After an odd character named Ledyard disappointed him Jefferson got Congress to finance the Lewis and Clark Expedition which opened up this continent as far as the Pacific coast. In Meriwether Lewis' journals, interspersed with his exact notations on the flora and fauna he encountered is the reiterated statement that he feels as if he were "in a dream." He died—either murdered or a suicide—in the wilds of Tennessee, in a dream, or perhaps in the "daze" you speak of in *Creative Intuition.* I am using him as a character in my new book and what you say in C. I. about the awe and challenge of wild Nature, "the vague and indeterminate potentialities . . . the infinite disproportion between Nature and man" is a kind of confirmation of something I've been struggling to dramatize. You get this feeling often in the records of early travels in this country.

And while I'm at it, may I compliment you on your English? It's terrific!

1. The date is penciled in, presumably by Maritain.
2. Jacques Maritain, *The Responsibility of the Artist* (New York, 1960).

3. Gordon never finished "A Narrow Heart: The Portrait of a Woman," an autobiographical novel that Veronica Makowsky, in *Caroline Gordon: A Biography,* 218, says eventually grew into *The Glory of Hera* (1972) and "The Joy of the Mountains." Gordon worked on it for more than twenty years.

4. Vera died December 31, 1959.

59

JACQUES MARITAIN TO CAROLINE GORDON

26 Linden Lane
Princeton, N.J.
April 9, 1960

Dear Caroline:

I treasure your letter. Pardon me for not having answered earlier. I was *too* tired and too full of worries.

The great generosity (and indulgence) with which you speak to me of my little book encourages me, and I am particularly grateful for this encouragement, because, for the time being, God is making me feel acutely what an ass I am.

You read me talentedly,—and charitably. So much so that you are complimenting me on my English. Now I shall tell you the truth: I *don't know* English. I am a blind man handling an instrument which he cannot see nor master. Thus what I can enjoy in the whole business is but my foolishness.

Raïssa and I are deeply touched by your compassion in our bereavement. Thank you for having attended with dear Francis the requiem mass for Vera. The void caused by her physical absence is unsurmountable.

Raïssa was quite unwell for many weeks—She is a little better now. We hope to see you after Easter, then perhaps the situation at home will be less miserable.

Pray for us, dear Caroline.

Our love to you
Jacques

I was greatly interested by your "Historical Note" about your great great great grandfather. I hope that your new book is near completion.

---------- 60 ----------

ALLEN TATE TO JACQUES MARITAIN

2019 Irving Ave. So.
Minneapolis 5, Minn
October 19, 1960

My dear Jacques,

Nini Borgerhoff has written me the distressing news of Raïssa.[1] My heart goes out to you. My own circumstances you know about, and I have delayed writing to you in the hope I should have the occasion to talk to you. I pray that Raïssa will sufficiently regain her strength to make it possible for you to bring her "home" soon. My affection for you both, inarticulate in the past year, never changes, nor does my gratitude for what you have both done for me. I shall be praying for you daily. My particular love to Raïssa.

Affectionately,
Allen

1. Raïssa suffered a stroke in the summer of 1960. Borgerhoff's letter (dated October 9, 1960) is printed in Appendix A.

---------- 61 ----------

JACQUES MARITAIN TO ALLEN TATE

36 rue de Varenne
Paris
October 21, 1960

My very dear Allen:

Your letter touched me deeply and I thank you for it whole-heartedly.

You know how lovingly and unceasingly Raïssa and I have been thinking of you.

For three months God has cast us into the abyss. Now Raïssa is weakening more each day and the doctor no longer leaves me any hope at all. She has the peace of God in her heart, her eyes have an overwhelming beauty, she has more greatness than ever. But it is a terrible thing to see the one you love more than everything in the world going slowly and inexorably toward death by dent of weakness. Pray for her, Allen, pray much for her. And pray a little for me, useless wretch that I am. Our abiding love to you.

Affectionately,
Jacques [1]

1. Borgerhoff's October 24, 1960, letter to Tate, giving details of Raïssa's last few weeks, is printed in Appendix A.

62

CAROLINE GORDON TO JACQUES MARITAIN

The Red House
Ewing Street
Princeton, New Jersey
October 23, 1960

Dear Jacques:

I have been travelling for months now towards a sort of imaginary rendez-vous with you: something you wrote in your book about America expresses so wonderfully the feeling that my ill-starred cousin, the explorer, Meriwether Lewis, seems to have had all his life.....But now I must think of you and Raissa as being in Paris and in great distress. Nini has been so kind about giving your friends here the news of Raissa and of you. My heart goes out to you both. I think of you both so very often and I wish I could do something to help—but I can only send my love and offer my heart-felt prayers for you both,

as ever,
Caroline

—————————————————————— 63 ——————————————————————

ALLEN TATE TO JACQUES MARITAIN

2019 Irving Avenue South
Minneapolis 5, Minnesota
November 11, 1960

My dear Jacques,

I did not see the New York Times and only yesterday a letter from Cornelia Borgerhoff brought news of Raïssa's death.[1]

I have prayed daily for Raïssa and for you ever since I heard of her illness, and I shall continue to pray.

My heart goes out to you, dear Jacques. I anxiously await news of your plans. But you must husband your strength: I shall learn your plans from Mrs. Borgerhoff.

If Raïssa must linger in Purgatory at all, her time there will be brief. I wish I were near you. My love and prayers.

Allen

1. Raïssa died November 4, 1960.

—————————————————————— 64 ——————————————————————

JACQUES MARITAIN TO ALLEN TATE

[*On a printed card expressing thanks for sympathy in grief*].

Prob. November 1960[1]

My very dear Allen, I thank you for your letter wholeheartedly. During the four months of her illness, the ordeal was terrible. But the peace of God was always deep in her, in the profound silence in which He emprisoned her. Her eyes and her smile, her beauty were more splendid than ever. To Peter van der Meer, who came from Holland to see her (he is a monk now) she said: "Personne ne peut m'aider."[2] Now she will help us. Her body is in the cemetery of a little village in Alsace, Kolbsheim.[3] Pray for her, pray for me. Je vous embrasse de tout mon coeur

Votre pauvre
Jacques[4]

1. The date was penciled in later, presumably by Tate.
2. "No one can help me." Peter van der Meer was a Dutch editor who collaborated with Maritain at the Desclée de Brouwer publishing house in Paris.
3. Maritain's body was also laid to rest in the cemetery of this village, where his friends Alexandre and Antoinette Grunelius lived. Their château now houses the Cercle d'Etudes Jacques et Raïssa Maritain.
4. "I embrace you with all my heart . . . Your poor Jacques."

65

ALLEN TATE TO JACQUES MARITAIN

2019 Irving Avenue South
Minneapolis 5, Minnesota
November 28, 1960

My dear Jacques,

Cornelia Borgerhoff writes me that you are flying back on the 30th to stay a month or perhaps five weeks, but that you expect to live in France in future. I have been anxious about your worldly arrangements: who will look after you? I know that you have family and old friends in France; so I am sure your decision is the right one. But what a loss your absence will be for us—for *me* even though miles have separated us for years. Your wisdom and grace nevertheless have sustained me, and of course will continue to do so even though the distance will be greater.

I wish there were a prospect of my being in Princeton before you leave. I can scarcely believe that, after your ordeal, you will be equal to coming to Chicago and South Bend for your annual lectures. But if you do come, I shall fly to Chicago to see you.

I pray for Raïssa and for you, my dear friend, morning and night, and you are in my heart all day.

My love to you,
Allen

--------------------------- 66 ---------------------------

JACQUES MARITAIN TO ALLEN TATE

26 Linden Lane
Princeton, N.J.
6 Décembre 1960

Allen, mon très cher Allen,

Merci de votre si bonne et douce lettre. Si vous saviez comme votre affection m'est chère, et comme elle était, *est* chère à Raïssa![1]

Allen, during four months I was on the verge of despair. Raïssa saved me from it. In profound silence her soul radiated peace and love and union with God. Julian Green saw her very often (he lives in the same street), and each time he said he had received some divine joy from her.

She fortifies me now. But I am wounded forever. Of course I cannot lecture in Chicago and South Bend! But I hope that every year I shall be able to spend some weeks in this country, not to teach or lecture, but to see my friends. Then I shall see you, and embrace you, my dear Allen.

For the time being, I am removing all our things from our house, which I shall try to rent. Thereafter I shall live sometimes in Alsace (in Kolbsheim, where her body has been buried), sometimes in Toulouse, with the Petits Frères de Jésus (je reste un laïque, mais je me suis mis à leur service et ils m'ont accepté).[2] I wish to be a poor among them.

You are always present to my heart. If you come to France during the summer, don't fail to pay a visit to me and my friends Grunelius in Kolbsheim (near Strasbourg).

Pray for Raïssa, pray for me.

My love to you,
Jacques

1. "Thank you for your good, sweet letter. If you knew how dear your affection is to me, and how it was, *is* to Raïssa!"

2. "I remain a layman, but I have put myself at their service and they have accepted me." See note 16 of the Introduction.

67

ALLEN TATE TO JACQUES MARITAIN

c/o American Express Co.
Florence, Italy
5th June 1961

My dear Jacques,

This letter will precede the arrival in Toulouse of a distinguished American painter, William Congdon, who is a cousin of my wife Isabella.[1]

William was converted two years ago, and is now bringing to bear upon his art the full significance of his new life. He is planning a book which he wants to talk to you about.

I take this opportunity to say that I very much want to write something about Raïssa, perhaps for the Sewanee Review. But I no longer own any of her books of poems. I have only *Les Grandes Amitiés* and *La Situation de la Poésie*.[2]

Please let me know how you are. Robert Speaight told me in London that you were well, and I rejoyced [*sic*].[3]

We return to America on June 14th and shall be at Wellfleet, Mass. for the summer.

My love to you dear Jacques,

Allen

1. Isabella Stewart Gardner was Tate's second wife.
2. Raïssa Maritain, *Les Grandes Amitiés: Souvenirs* (New York, 1941); and, in collaboration with Jacques Maritain, *La Situation de la poésie* (Paris, 1938).
3. Robert Speaight (1904–76) was a British actor and author. He wrote biographies of French writers, including Georges Bernanos and François Mauriac.

68

JACQUES MARITAIN TO ALLEN TATE

Toulouse
June 9, 1961

My very dear Allen,

I just wrote to you c/o American Express, hoping my letter can reach you in Florence before your departure.

I myself am leaving Toulouse tomorrow, so, much to my regret, William Congdon will not find me here. I hope he will speak with the Petits Frères and like them. I told them of his possible arrival. One of them is himself a (good) painter. Willard Hill, who is an American, may guide the cousin of your wife among the Little Brothers.

The fact that you are planning to write something about Raissa is for me immensely moving and all-important. I shall be in KOLBSHEIM (Bas-Rhin) on June 23. Please write me there, telling me *at what address* I must send you Raissa's books of poems. I shall do it as soon as I receive your letter. Robert Speaight will probably be at Kolbsheim at the same time.

With my love to you, dearest Allen,

As ever yours,
Jacques
My kind regards to your wife.

69

JACQUES MARITAIN TO ALLEN TATE

Kolbsheim
(Bas-Rhin)
25 June 1961

My very dear Allen,

I saw William Congdon in Paris. I have a great liking for him and I believe from the photos he showed me that he is a very good painter. I also believe that he should not let himself be "used" too much by over-zealous friends and that he should do religious painting only when he feels an irresistible inner urge to do so. I am going to try to write a preface for his book.[1] The only question for me is to find the necessary time, but I think I'll be able to.

Mr. Congdon confirmed for me that your present address in the United States is simply: Wellfleet, Mass. So that's where I'm sending you four of Raïssa's books: *Night Letter, In the Clefts of the Rock, Gates of the Horizon*, and *Story of Abraham*.[2] (I believe you already have *Situation of Poetry*). You know how much your article will mean to me.

You will find enclosed a memorial that I had made for Raïssa and another for Vera. The two verses of Saint John of the Cross that I put on

Raïssa's are ones that she repeated constantly for months before being stricken by the disease that suddenly separated her from the world of men and of their language, leaving to it only the "ardent lamp in her heart," and shattering everything for me.

Pray for me. Affectionately,
Jacques

1. William Congdon, *In My Disk of Gold* (New York, 1962).

2. Raïssa Maritain, *Lettre de nuit, La Vie dornée* (Montreal, 1943); *Au creux du rocher* (Paris, 1954; *Portes de l'horizon/Doors of the Horizon* (Bethlehem, Conn., 1952); *Histoire d'Abraham* (Paris, 1947).

70

CAROLINE GORDON TO JACQUES MARITAIN

The Red House
Ewing Street
Princeton, New Jersey
December 24, 1961

Dear Jacques:

Here is a book mark for you. The peacock feathers came from Flannery O'Connor's peacocks. The art work is one of those skills taught in kindergartens. Amy, Nancy's youngest, is being taught Algebra, along with these skills, but hasn't yet been permitted to learn her letters! (Sic.) [1]

Nancy came by the other day with a Christmas present for me which she admired so that she couldn't wait till Christmas to give it to me! It is one of those photographs of you which Ulli Stelzer [*sic*] made while you were here in October. [2] I like it as much as she does and am happy to have it. I am sending a print of the same photograph to Fr. Charles, the librarian at the Monastery of the Holy Ghost at Conyers, Georgia. (James Conyers was the boy who guided Wesley into that part of the country, then wilderness.) Father Charles—originally one of the most dissolute young men who ever came Dorothy Day's way, she says—is a great admirer of yours and of Raïssa's and will be very happy to have it.

These monks have sort of adopted Flannery O'Connor and me as pipe-lines to the outer world. A poor choice, in each case, it would seem. Still, we both know people who can do the things they want done even if we can't do them ourselves—and their plan seems to work.

I spent Wednesday night three weeks ago in the brownstone mansion on East Seventy Second Street owned by my former boss at the New School and asked the maid who let me in if she could find me a detective story (for it is my abominable habit to read myself to sleep.) She replied austerely that Miss Mayer had put some "literature" in my room.[3]

The literature was two books: Salinger's *Franny and Zooey* which I ought to read for professional reasons but which I have kept putting off reading because I knew beforehand what it would be: the wisdom contained in that nineteenth century boot-legging of excerpts from *The Philokalia*, (called *The Way of the Pilgrim*,) bobbing up at a Princeton house party and on East Seventy Second Street. The other book was another life of Charles de Foucauld, by Marion Mill Premminger [*sic*].[4] She and Albert Mayer were married two months ago and the bride and groom and sister in law take off for Africa in January.[5]

Miss Mayer was only half way through her sister in law's book but resumed its reading with greater zest when I told her I had a friend who had lately become a member of that order which did not have a single member in Charles de Foucauld's life time! I'm so proud of you!

She also undertook to "tape," herself, or get taped, records of certain discussions at the New School which might be the kind of thing the Trappists want.

The pipe line is working not too badly at this end—Miss Mayer is just the helper for those monks. It is also a wonderful channel of grace from the monastery. Nancy's other piece of news, again so good she couldn't keep it to herself, was that she was "determined" to send Caroline and Amy to the school which the sisters of the Sacred Heart will open here soon—and, as a friend of mine exclaimed: "None too soon!"

I have asked a lot of people to pray for this and am not surprised. The ways of God are, of course, incomprehensible but occasionally one seems to catch a glimpse of the working of God's will. Caroline has demanded that she be allowed to practise some religion so in the past few months poor Percy, (who really works too hard, with a private practise in addition to his hospital work,) heaves himself out of bed at nine o'clock on Sunday mornings to take Amy to the Episcopal Sunday School. (The little girls naturally have to go at different hours.)

Caroline speaks sometimes of .... "If we ever get Amy baptized" and I surmise that she has been asking her parents why Amy shouldn't go the same way her parents want her to. I also surmise that those poor children, Nancy and Percy, Catholic still at heart (I have always felt that Percy would make the best Christian of the lot of us in time!) those poor little strayed creatures cannot bring themselves to subject Amy to an heretical rite or participate in one themselves. All surmise, of course, but I do know that Nancy is pretty confused; Allen tells her that he is still in the Church.

That is about all the news from the House of Tatreus. I am awfully mythologically minded these days because of a class I have at the New School. Our task is the identification of the fundamental principles which under-lie all competent fictions. Our subject matter is the plays of Aeschylus, Sophocles and Euripides. Two of each, if we can make it, during the year. So far we have put all our time on the *Oresteia*. It has nearly worked me to death but has been a lot of fun and a lot of help in my own work.

I am sending you under separate cover the second chapter of the novel I am working on.[6] I do not approve of college magazines. I think the young gentlemen would be better off studying the works of any dead masters rather than considering the work of any live master. But I published this chapter in *Shenandoah* because it was founded by a young critic who, taking off, he tells me from some passages of your work, has written a study of my work which he is calling *The Lesson of the Masters*. One chapter, "The Novel As Christian Comedy," evidently owes its inspiration to you.[7] It is an exposition of the idea that *The Divine Comedy* is a synthesis of *genres*, already existing in Dante's time, which may be found in any serious work of fiction.

As for me, as a novelist, I continue to follow, even at a considerable distance, in your foot-steps. You have had very little to say about the novel as an art form but those few specific remarks contain profound insights and are the most practical help that I, as a novelist, have had.

Dear Jacques, don't bother to answer this letter. I sink sometimes under the weight of my own correspondence—and don't even like to think what a heavy burden *yours* is!

We were all so happy to have you here in October and will hope and pray that you come again. In the meantime it is wonderful to know that you are happy in your work there,

> with love and prayers, always,
> Caroline

One more bit of news from the Tates. I have a new extra-curricular pupil: my last psychiatrist! Now that I realize I can't help Allen except by praying for him, I have been enjoying certain pleasures I couldn't enjoy formerly. One of them is not having to frequent psychiatrists. This dear soul evidently misunderstood Allen's oft-reiterated remark that I have as little intellect as any human being he ever encountered. He felt that if I would only read St. Thomas more things would go better. I did try—but simply couldn't take it in. (Allen is so right about that!)

This doctor finally persuaded me that it was my duty to see him. He really has talent! Writes well—indeed, better than most of his English speaking colleagues—and has some interesting literary insights .... If you live long enough, you certainly see some funny things, don't you?

I wish I could have written this in French—but would be harder reading than it is. I wrote my first novel in Paris—one of the many reasons why my French is practically non-existent. But I love hearing it spoken and I imagine that it is a great joy to you to hear it spoken all around you every day.

1. The *sic* is Gordon's.

2. Ulli Steltzer (1923—) is a German-born photographer who won the British Columbia Book Award in 1980 for *Coast of Many Faces* (Seattle, 1979).

3. The New School was a private university located in Greenwich Village, founded in 1919 by a group that included John Dewey. Clara Woollie Mayer was vice-president of the New School from 1950 to 1961.

4. Marion Mill Preminger (1913–72) was a Viennese-born actress whose first husband was director Otto Preminger. A disciple of Albert Schweitzer, she helped treat lepers with him and lectured in the United States to raise funds for his hospital in the Congo.

5. Mayer's brother Albert (1897–1981) was a world-renowned architect and housing planner.

6. Caroline Gordon, "The Dragon's Teeth," *Shenandoah,* XIII (1961), 22–34. This story must have become part of *The Glory of Hera.*

7. The chapter, by Ashley Brown, was published in *Reality and Myth: Essays in American Literature in Honor of Richmond Croom Beatty,* ed. William E. Walker and Robert L. Welker (Nashville, 1964).

71

CAROLINE GORDON TO JACQUES MARITAIN

The Red House
Ewing Street
Princeton, New Jersey
Nov. 2, 1964

Dear Jacques:

It was so heartening to see you at the Morses's the other day! I wish you could stay over here longer but I know you have commitments in France. We need you here, too, though!

I believe I told you hurriedly that I am thinking of leaving my "literary remains" to the Raissa Maritain Library? If you think that is a good plan I will go out one day soon and talk with Mother Kirby and the Librarians.[1]

My stuff is of no great value but I *have* lived long enough to have known a great many people! Nowadays an aging writer like me has a hard time getting her work done because of the young professors who are writing books about writers. It seems to me that every other day some young man turns up, wanting to know something about Hart Crane or William Faulkner or Ford Madox Ford or Scott Fitzgerald. The young profs *have* to write these books in order to get promotion but it is getting to be almost a racket and very time-consuming for people who want to get any writing done themselves. At any rate, one reason for leaving my stuff to the library at Stuart Hall is the chance that some earnest young writer may meet Mother Kirby or some of the other Sisters of the Sacred Heart and, consequently, have a little light thrown on his pathway.

I'm enclosing a chapter of the novel I'm writing. Don't bother to return it and read it at your leisure, please. The book purports to be an autobiography but is actually a novel.[2] The action takes place in modern times but the protagonist is Heracles—which presents some stiff technical problems, as you can see. I have been collecting data on Heracles (as a prototype of Christ) for a good many years now and have come on some astonishing things. I have occasionally felt that my interpretation of Heracles' life—and times—may be fanciful—until I read Fr. Hugo Rahner's *The Greek Myths and the Christian Mystery* last year.

Must get back to work. I have to write an essay on Flannery O'Connor for an anthology two professors are getting out. (The professors are all so busy writing books one wonders how they get any teaching done. The answer in most cases is that they don't.) I thought I knew Flannery's work as well as anybody—she has sent me her stories for comment for years. I re-read them all in preparation for this essay. I find—to my surprise—that she has more in common with Henry James than almost any other American writer.

Dear Jacques, how I wish we could keep you on this side of the water! Take as good care of yourself as you can,

with love, always, and with heart-felt thanks for all you've done for me,

Caroline

1. The Stuart Country Day School in Princeton, New Jersey, is run by the Sisters of the Sacred Heart. Its library is dedicated to Raïssa Maritain and includes a collection of works

by Raïssa and Jacques Maritain. Perhaps its most notable holding is the original manuscript of their translation of Allen Tate's "Ode to the Confederate Dead."
2. Caroline Gordon, *The Glory of Hera* (Garden City, N.Y., 1972).

72

JACQUES MARITAIN TO CAROLINE GORDON

Princeton, N. J.
November 5, 64

Dear Caroline,

A thousand thanks for your sweet letter.

I was so moved and so glad to see you at the Morses',—and the little Caroline with you.

Because of my bad English (worse than ever) I was unable to tell you how touched I am by your intention to leave your "literary remains" to the R. M. Library. It is a testimony of love which is invaluable to my heart. I have no words for what I feel. Raïssa had—she has—so profound a love for this people (I mean the American people) and this country. And now there is in Princeton this love for her in return. There is a great blessing there. I am sure she will guide the work of those who will consult your precious documents,—young writers no doubt, and first of all students at the Stuart School, and teachers as well. And blessed be you, dear Caroline!

You FORGOT to enclose the promised chapter of your novel. Please send it to me as soon as possible, so that I may read it on the boat. (I am leaving Princeton on November 10). I am very curious about your Heracles. And send me in Toulouse your essay on Flannery O'Connor when it is printed.

I do hope that you will decide to write not only a sort of autobiography in the form of a novel, but your full memories.

Pray for me.

My love to you, dear Caroline. Devotedly yours, as ever

Jacques

CAROLINE GORDON TO JACQUES MARITAIN

The Red House
Ewing Street
Princeton, New Jersey
Saturday

Dear Jacques:

I am so glad you approve my plans for my "papers." I feel with you that Raissa *will* guide the work of young people who come to the library for research. One of the most spectacular conversions I have ever heard of came about as the result of a young scientist having to go [to] the library of a Benedictine monastery for some research. He told me that up to that time it had not occurred to him that Benedictine monks could read, much less write!

I enclose a chapter of this novel I am working on. I, myself, am so burdened with the reading of other people's manuscripts these days I hesitated to send it to you. However, I believe that you will be sympathetic to the theme, and not only because, like all of my writings of recent years, it owes its inspiration to your work. I suppose the book is an attempt at a dramatization of something you have written: "Who touches a transcendental touches Being."

I hope to have the life of Heracles wind antiphonally, as it were, throughout my chronicle. He is the only one of the Greek heroes who "went to heaven," you will recall. There are echoes of the *Magnificat* in the directions Tiresias gives for the sprinkling of the serpents' ashes on "the rock the Sphinx" perched on. The first mortal woman with whom Zeus lay—Niobe—turned out a *mater dolorosa*. Heracles had a reverence for virginity; King Thespius was afraid that his fifty daughters might provide him with unworthy grandsons so, while Heracles was hunting the Nemean lion by day he slept each night with one of the king's daughters—all except one. One daughter declined to share the hero's bed, preferring to remain a virgin. Heracles honoured her by making her the priestess of the first temple he erected in honour of his father, Zeus. Like all the Greek demi-gods he smarted under the accusation of being a bastard and was always praying to his father for recognition. The only time Zeus ever condescended to speak with him was in the Temple of Jupiter Ammon at Thebes and he disguised himself there by covering himself with a ram's fleece and speaking through a ram's lips! ... As you see, I've got some fine material. Now if I can only be equal to it!

I hope to make something rather nice out of Eurystheus. A sort of fore-runner of the contemporary writer, I suspect. Writing his autobiography, probably, in that brazen urn he had fashioned for himself, just far enough beneath the earth's surface for him not to be made nervous by Heracles' giant foot-steps. You will recall that Eurystheus made a law that none of Heracles' trophies should be brought "inside the gates." The smell of blood made him nervous!

But your practised eye will already have taken the measure of the task that confronts me. Again I say: If I can only measure up to it! I figure that I have about three—maybe five—more years of intensive work in me, so, as you can see, I have no time to waste.

Dear Jacques, thank you so much for your letter. It was very heartening and heartening above all to see you again. I do pray for you every day. I know you will give me a prayer often, too, and I cannot tell you what that means to me,

with love and deep gratitude,

Caroline

I will send you my piece on Flannery when I get it written.

74

JACQUES MARITAIN TO CAROLINE GORDON

Princeton, N.J.
10 November 64

Dear Caroline,

Just a word to thank you for sending me the chapter, which I shall be happy to read on the boat. Happy, yes, but with fear and trembling. For I am totally ignorant of Heracles and his story, and your science about him stuns me with awe.

Upon my farewell visit to the Stuart School, I spoke to Mother Kirby of your plan, which touched her greatly. Thank you again with all my heart, dear Caroline, I feel strongly that you are giving this very precious gift not only to the Library but also and primarily to Raïssa!

Affectionately,
Jacques

CAROLINE GORDON TO JACQUES MARITAIN

The Red House
Ewing Street
Princeton, New Jersey
September 29, 1965

Dear Jacques:

I think of you and Raïssa and Vera very often, of course, but lately I think of you even oftener as I am spending my afternoons, from four o'clock on, with your *Note-Books*.[1] I spend my mornings mostly with Jean Cauvin (in the line of duty.) By noon time my nature is quite soured. It is wonderful to be able to look forward to pleasanter and more rewarding association in the afternoons.

I had to read Abel LeFranc's *La Jeunesse du Calvin* in French. This exhausted my linguistic powers so I am getting a friend to read me your Note-Books in a running translation. He is a retired professor of French (did his thesis on Remy de Gourmont) and a man of Encyclopedic knowledge, Albert Lippman. He seems to enjoy the readings as much as I do.

I have had to sort of divide my "papers" between the Library of the University and the Raissa Maritain Library. This is because I had to have some expert help from Alexander Clark and was ashamed to have received their hospitality all these years without making any return. However, I have already begun to deposit some papers out at the Sacred Heart. One item is a series of letters from Katherine Anne Porter which really form a kind of travelogue. She was always moving from place to place and when she got to a new place sat down and spent some of the creative energy she should have used in her work in letters to me and other friends. I also intend to deposit the notes for this novel I am working on at the Raissa Maritain.[2] They weigh twenty pounds and include notes on the lives of Calvin, Lord Byron, Meriwether Lewis (my cousin,) Thomas Jefferson (who had my great great grandfather for his first teacher,) my great great uncle, the famous Dr. Hunter, (the first man to dissect a whale,) John Locke and the Lord knows how many other worthies. They should make edifying reading. At any rate, I hope the deposits will serve the purpose we both have at heart to lead people not of the faith to Raïssa who will, as you say, lead them to Christ.

I feel, too, that having to divide the papers is, perhaps, Providential as it establishes a link between the two libraries. Bill Dix and Alexander Clark have been most sympathetic and helpful.

I feel, too, that being able to keep company with the youthful Maritain of afternoons may be Providential. I have been swimming in mighty deep waters for the past ten years and need any help I can get!

This letter needs no answer. You know how many people in Princeton are thinking of you and would send their love if they knew I was writing. I send my love and, as always my heart-felt thanks, for all you have done for us,

Caroline

After more reading: I have always felt that Proust was right when he said that the work of art already exists—timelessly—and that the artist's task is chiefly one of translation or transference. The transference of the fragments of this work of art must have been a delicate and arduous labour. It is certainly beautiful. Again, love and thanks,

C.

1. Jacques Maritain, *Carnets de notes* (Paris, 1965).
2. See No. 58, note 3.

76

CAROLINE GORDON TO JACQUES MARITAIN

The Red House
Ewing Street
Princeton, New Jersey
Feb. 11, 1968

Dearest Jacques:

I know you must be deluged with fan mail about—as well as protests against—your new book.[1] But I feel impelled to make my own contribution.

I cannot tell you how glad I am that you have written this book. I, for one, don't know how I could have got along much longer without it. And there must be a lot of other people in my plight.

I have been distressed by certain aspects of the *Aggiornamento*. Among them the bad translations of the Epistles and the Gospels. But chiefly, the exaltation—in many quarters—of private opinion. Wasn't it Pere Grou who said that it was the oldest malady of the human race?

One reason I have been so distressed is that I have spent the last ten years much in the company of John Calvin and some of his *confrères*. It has seemed to me that a lot of the notions that got lodged in their heads have been swarming over us nowadays. At times I have actually been frightened by the torrent of muddy thought which has been pouring over us. I know, of course, that it is foolish to be frightened; the Church will prevail. But it is wonderful to be reassured, as I have been reassured, by your book!

I do not and never will understand all you say in any of your books but I got enough out of *The Peasant* to make me feel equal to carrying on, in my work and in my daily life.

I particularly admire the chapter called "The Liberation of the Intelligence." And I do not see how I could have got along much longer without the section on "Teilhard and Teilhardism."[2] I have long suspected that "Teilhardism" was one more Christian gnosis but to have it nailed down as "a *theology-fiction*" has been a great help to me.

I have just finished a piece in which I tried to compare the last story in Flannery O'Connor's post-humous volume, *Everything That Rises Must Converge*, with the several versions of Flaubert's *Temptations de Saint Antoine* [*sic*].[3] It seems to me that Flannery succeeded where the great Flaubert failed, chiefly, because she confined herself to a portrayal of the operations of one heresy whereas Flaubert had nineteen or twenty parade past Saint Anthony.

Robert Fitzgerald, in his introduction to Flannery's volume of short stories, comments on the fact that her title comes from Teilhard de Chardin. He says:

> It is a title taken in full respect and with profound and necessary irony. For Teilhard's vision of 'the omega point' virtually at the end of time, or at any rate of a time-span rightly conceivable by paleontologist or geologist alone, has appealed to people to whom it may seem to offer one more path past the Crucifixion.[4]

I have felt that what he says here is true but I feel this even more strongly after reading your book.

I went to Greece last September—for the first time—and stayed two and a half months. While I was there I was in quite a valedictory mood, saying of every landscape I fancied, "Well, I don't suppose I'll ever see *that* again." Now I'm back in Princeton I am scheming to get back to Greece one more time, at least. It almost seems necessary as I am still struggling with Herakles as the proto-type of the Christian soul. Fr. Hugo Rahner's *The Greek Myths and the Christian Mysteries* has been a great help to me as he seems to be trying to correct the Euhemerism of our times which, I think, Robert Graves represents.

The Woods grow a little older. Peto is twenty two, majoring in Spanish at Sewanee and much in love with a Minnesota girl named Heppelfinger. Young Allen is also at Sewanee and having a hard time. Neither of the boys have been properly educated and college is more difficult for them than it might have been if they had had a solid preparation. But they are good, fundamentally sweet-natured boys.

Allen has retired from regular teaching but continues to astonish— and at times appal [sic]—his friends and family. He and Isabella are divorced and he has married a twenty six year old girl who is a trained nurse and a former nun.[5] They have just produced twins! It is no joke to produce twins in your sixty ninth year and even Allen seems a little dashed by their arrival. I have great hopes of these twins, though. I believe that they are going to do great things for Allen—they have already acquainted him with some of the facts of life which have hitherto eluded him. But what an exacting role for the poor little things .... Still, lots of people are praying for them.

I sent little Allen a copy of your book the other day, urging him to read the chapter on "The Liberation of the Intelligence."

I can't mention all the things about the book that delighted me but the appellation "Chronolatry" is one. Also "Ideosophy." Those labels have been sorely needed.

Dear Jacques, you know, of course, how sadly you are missed in Princeton. Of course your friends all hope you'll get over this Fall. In the meantime, we have The Peasant with us. I just love the old fellow— perhaps because I am more fitted to associate with him than with M. Maritain!

as ever yours, with love from Nancy and Percy, too,

Caroline Tate

Flaubert ends his 1874 version of *The Temptation* with a Teilhardian vision of the universe! (As you doubtless recall.)

1. Jacques Maritain, *Le Paysan de la Garonne: Un Vieux Laïc s'interroge à propos du temps présent* (Paris, 1967). Gordon probably read it in translation: *The Peasant of the Garonne: An Old Layman Questions Himself About the Present Time*, trans. Michael Cuddihy and Elizabeth Hughes (New York, 1968).

2. Pierre Teilhard de Chardin (1881–1955) was a French priest and paleontologist whose writings sought a synthesis of Darwinian evolution and Christian theology.

3. Caroline Gordon, "Heresy in Dixie," *Sewanee Review*, LXXVI (1968), 263–97.

4. Robert Fitzgerald, Introduction to Flannery O'Connor's *Everything That Rises Must Converge* (New York, 1956), xxx.

5. Gordon is referring to Helen Heinz, whom Tate met in Minnesota in 1964.

77

JACQUES MARITAIN TO CAROLINE GORDON

Toulouse, 24 February 68

Dearest Caroline,

Thank you with all my heart for your good letter, which I read with so much pleasure and gratitude.

I am delighted with what you say about *Peasant*. You are quite right about Calvin and his brethren: "A lot of the notions that got lodged in their heads have been swarming over us nowadays." As for Teilhardism, it is a joy for me that we are in agreement on that. I have not read Flannery O'Connor's posthumous volume, but I like very much the passage by Robert Fitzgerald that you quoted. I do hope you'll send me your study of Flaubert and Flannery when it appears.

I envy your trip to Greece!

And thank you also for the news you give me on Peto and on young Allen. The news about Allen is great. With these two twins born of a former nun, the picture is complete. This great poet whom I love so much is an astounding force of nature. God will pardon him because God loves poets. But we really must pray for him.

Dear Caroline, I think of Princeton with nostalgia, but I do fear that I shall not ever be able to return. I'm about to be 86 years old and I'm *dog-tired*. And the more tired I get, the more I work; and the more I work, the more tired I get. But Raïssa guides me and supports me. Cowardice is so universally great (having a *bad image* is more dreadful to most people than being burned at the stake) that one is obliged to say what one can as long as one can. And I am trying to "open doors" ... (I'm sending you a little article just published in *Nova et Vetera*, Cardinal Journet's journal, which will perhaps interest you).[1]

Pray for me, dear Caroline.

My love to Nancy and Percy.

As ever yours,
Jacques

1. Jacques Maritain, "Faisons-lui une aide semblable à lui," *Nova et Vetera*, No. 4 (1967), 241–54.

CAROLINE GORDON TO JACQUES MARITAIN

The Red House
145 Ewing Street
Princeton
March 12, 1968

Dear Jacques:

It is evident to me that your youth has been prolonged like the eagle's so that you may circle above and keep the roads of contemplation open. I feel quite sure of this and you must feel it in your interior bones. I am sorry that you are so fatigued—but not astonished. You are a philosopher but you read literature as if you were a poet. You have laboured incessantly on two fronts all your life. It is no wonder you are fatigued!

Your essay arrived the other day. I have read it once or rather I got a friend who translates from the French effortlessly to read it to me and I will read it again—in my own slow fashion. This essay comes in mighty handy for me. I have been floundering about among archetypes for some years now. It is difficult and dangerous work. Raïssa's insight about the composition of Woman is terrific. It is obvious once it is pointed out but that never occurred to me although I have often reflected on the fact that while Woman is chthonic in all mythologies, the soul is always feminine.

I was interested by what you said about Titanism in *The Peasant.* I believe that it is resurgent in our time. Perhaps it was never far beneath the ground. I have many friends who have written books on Herman Melville but so far as I know not one of them has mentioned what seems to me [the] essential characteristic of his work: Titanism. In one sentence in *Moby Dick* he piles Ossa on Pelion, as it were—that is, he reverses the mythological order and makes Uranus (Heaven) feminine when he writes: "The fair, *girlish* forehead of the sky." You and I have a friend who sometimes strikes the same note. Allen writes: "Man, dull critter of enormous head / What would he look for in the coiling sky?"

I was two thirds through your book when I wrote you that "fan" letter. Now I have finished it I can say something I couldn't say before. I greatly admire the *shape* of the book. It seems to me a bold act of the imagination. You begin theologically, shift to the philosophical level and end poetically, that is to say, with a fusion of the three levels. Or it seems to me.

You couldn't have done this without Raissa's help, as you say. Still, you have used that help *poetically*, in a truly creative way. The achievement is certainly impressive—and timely. One is sometimes tempted to think that in our day the roads of contemplation have been fenced off (as "dead ends,"). At any rate, many people feel that they cannot be travelled in our own times. (I verily believe that our friend, Francis Fergusson, would be in the Church if he understood the doctrine of the Communion of Saints. I judge that he doesn't, from remarks he has made to me.) Raïssa, as you say, guides you and watches over you. In this book you have made it possible for her to guide others. I am very happy for you both.

I sent *The Peasant* to little Allen (who is now twenty, a Junior at Sewanee) and, like his brother, pretty bewildered. Percy assumed a heavy responsibility when he took the whole family out of the Church. But I believe they will all make it back (including Percy.) Allen Wood writes: Dear Grandma:

Thank you for your letter and *The Peasant of the Garonne.* I shall try to read it over spring vacation. The gift of this book is most timely, because recently I have found that the only questions that can hold my attention are ones of a spiritual nature. Religion is, for the first time in my life, becoming a primary concern. I find that I am not so much worried by the whys of belief or worship but by the hows. How does one worship God?

Isn't that letter touching?

Here are two pieces of news that may interest you from your adopted country (which I know you keep in touch with through other correspondents.) But Eugene McCarthy's candidacy seems to me one of the most important things that has happened in our time. The New York Times ignored or misrepresented his candidacy until they were practically forced to acknowledge it by the columnists. I enclose an editorial they had a few days ago. We knew McCarthy and his wife in Minnesota. They are wonderful people. Gene is, doubtless, the best educated man in American politics. He is a devout Catholic—has taken St. Thomas More as his patron. Everybody says he can't possibly win and when he entered the race he said that it was probably political suicide. But a good many people are beginning to realize that he is attempting something that hasn't been attempted before. [You might almost say that he is creating a new political climate.] [1] God knows one is needed. I remember your saying once that you felt that the Little Brothers of Charles de Foucauld were the most significant movement in France. McCarthy, single-handed, seems to be trying to create a new political climate.

I must get to work,

love, as ever,

from

Caroline[2]

1. This sentence is marked through in the typescript.
2. Sister Marie Pascale acknowledged this letter on behalf of Maritain. Her letter is printed in Appendix A.

79

CAROLINE GORDON TO JACQUES MARITAIN

The Red House
Ewing Street
Princeton, New Jersey
October 25, 1969

Dear Jacques:

Before I forget, please don't ever feel that you have to answer any letter I write you. The last time I wrote I forgot to say that and, in consequence, you acknowledged my letter. That isn't necessary. I write because I wish I could see you and talk with me [sic] and also because, occasionally, I have something to say which, I think will interest you.

The first thing I have to say this time is that I believe I already perceive the impact which *The Peasant of the Garonne* is having—on all sorts of people. I have read it twice and am beginning my third reading. I tell everybody—who will listen that if they want to understand their own times they had better read this book.

I think I can give you an example of this. My daughter, Nancy, has become very political-minded. To the surprise of all of us she turns out to have a talent for raising money! She worked very hard for Eugene McCarthy when he was campaigning for president and like many of his adherents, felt a little dashed, (I suspect,) when he seemed to have retired from the field after he was defeated by Nixon. (Of course the poor man was working hard, writing a book—but, as *you* know, writing books isn't considered real work!) Nancy has been in Washington all the past week, agitating in behalf of the "moratorium," a nation-wide protest against the continuation of the war in Vietnam which has been observed on most college campusses. Nancy had lunch yesterday with Senator Mc-Carthy and came away with much food for thought, and, in addition, more whole-heartedly committed to work for him politically.

Their conversation, which lasted three hours, was mostly about angels—and angelism, she said. (At this point I was reminded of something you said in print years ago, that our chief danger was not from the atom bomb but from "angelism," man's effort to use his own intellect as if it were an angel's intellect.) McCarthy, whether or not the idea is original with him, seems to be in complete accord with you on that. He told Nancy that he expected Bobby Kennedy to come out against him a little later in the campaign but that he was astounded when Bobby announced his candidacy immediately after McCarthy made such a strong showing in New Hampshire. He holds in mind that men—and masses—frequently succumb to the guidance of their dark angels as well as their light angels and thinks that that is what Bobby did then.

Looking back on his own campaign, he feels that he made a mistake in campaigning in Harlem. That, of course, means back slapping, hand shaking and baby kissing. He said to Nancy, "You, as a Southerner will realize that later I felt that when I did that that I was patronizing the Negroes." I remember that in one of McCarthy's first key speeches he spoke briefly on the "Negro question," saying that we Americans had treated them the way the French and British had treated their Colonials and that we had better stop doing it before it was too late. He has a strong sense of history, rare among American politicians.

He has been writing poetry. Nancy (who knows what suffering the writing of poetry entails!) urged him to give it up. He protested, saying "But some of my new stuff is pretty good." Nancy said, "I don't care. I want you to be president." Whereupon he patted her hand and said, "I will." This statement made his earnest worker very happy, of course! He asked her, though, to give him six months of quiet "and then we will see what happens."

He said in the course of the conversation (what Henry James said in 1912 in *The American Scene*) that the future of this country rested in the hands of the American girl. While making this assertion James also described her whom he labelled "the terrible woman of the future"—what is nowadays called "a jet setter."

McCarthy has gone even a little farther than James in his insight, I believe. He characterizes our age as being predominantly "homosexual" and certainly manners, morals, customs, women's clothes offer evidence to that effect. He thinks all these trends point to a return of the influence of the Earth Mother, which, given time, will return us to the worship of our Heavenly *Father*, "hopefully," as they say these days. (You need more than a sense of history to go along with thinking as long range as this but I have felt for some time that the modern man when he turned his back on God eased his sense of guilt by pushing the little woman out front, saying, in effect, "Let her take the rap."[)] McCarthy, better grounded theologically and philosophically than I am, thinks that women will take a leading part in politics from now on. Particularly when it comes to the "Kill ratio," since their instinct, if not perverted, is to produce and preserve life rather than destroy it.

I have now made as faithful a report as I can of a conversation which I think will interest you and interested me because, for one thing, I observed so many of your ideas in circulation.

It must be a source of deep satisfaction to you, dear Jacques—if you ever take enough time off from working to reflect on it—that so many things you have said, after germinating under ground, so to speak, are suddenly flowering in a field that seems, on the surface, more weed-infested than other ages one might cite.

I am certainly glad I entered the Church when I did! The "new theology" has me baffled—or would if I didn't have your distinction between "hard core" and "soft core" ecumenism to fall back upon .... And our present Pope! My admiration for him grows daily.

Another distinction which you make in *The Peasant* is enormously helpful to me: That there are only two real philosophies in the world today: Christian philosophy and Marxist philosophy. Because of their respective, if fundamentally opposed, attitudes towards matter! The truth of what you say here becomes more apparent to me every day. Marxism has infiltrated our language to such an extent that, sometimes as I write, I stop to wonder if anybody will be able to read what I have written, so obsolescent now is what used to be called "a good prose style." It is fascinating—if horrifying—to observe the Marxisms in The New York Times news stories. I enclose a sample. Nancy is trying to learn to write what she labels "Politicalese." The other day she asked me to type some stuff for her, first warning me not to correct her grammar or her diction. I kept silent until she spoke of something as "the elitest." "You can't say that!" I protested. She said, "Mama, you just don't understand the use of that word. 'Elite' is now a verb. You say 'Quit eliting me!' "

What a lengthy letter! But remember you are not to bother to answer it. Your friends here all miss you dreadfully but you know that, of course.

But you have left us plenty of matter for contemplation. And I am starting today on my third reading of *The Peasant*,

with much love always,

Caroline

80

JACQUES MARITAIN TO CAROLINE GORDON

29 December 69

Dearest Caroline,

Thank you for your dear letter which deeply touched me. I can write only a few lines, being half dead of fatigue because of a book (on the Church) which I have undertaken to write and which is beyond my strength.[1] I am so happy that you like the *Peasant*! To you and to Nancy (what you tell me of her conversation with McCarthy interested me enormously) all my wishes for the new year, with the very faithful affection of old

Jacques

1. Jacques Maritain, *De l'église du Christ: La Personne de l'eglise et son personnel* (Paris, 1970). This was the last book Maritain published himself. The Cercle d'Etudes Jacques et Raïssa Maritain in Kolbsheim published a collection of his last writings posthumously: *Approches sans Entraves* (Paris, 1973).

Additional Letters

JACQUES MARITAIN TO FREDERICK MORGAN

26 Linden Lane
Princeton, N.J.
February 25, 1952

Mr. Frederick Morgan
c/o *The Hudson Review*
439 West Street
New York 14, N.Y.

Dear Mr. Morgan:

I thank you most cordially for your kind letter which reminds me of the pleasure I had in meeting you at the Tates', and which I have read with great interest.

I realize the importance of your project of a group of Catholic laymen, especially writers, dedicated to bear constructive and enlightened witness to cultural and intellectual values.

Yet, since you do me the honor, which touches me greatly, of asking my opinion,—I feel bound to tell you of my misgivings quite frankly. I don't like to give advice, but I am forced to do so by your kindness and confidence.

The point is that the activity of such a group may be conceived in two ways. The group may be conceived either as serving the personal work of Catholic writers *in their own creative way*, and as essentially interested in *artistic and intellectual activity*, and in awakening in Catholic opinion a greater awareness of the importance and dignity of the values which the writer and the artist serve and of free intellectual research. Or it may be conceived as essentially interested in a kind of political-religious testimony, external in itself to the activity of the writer or the artist, and as acting in the defense of a certain ideological program.

In my opinion the first conception answers a necessity of this time and would enable the group to exercize a most useful and fecund influence. The second conception, on the contrary, risks, I think, involving the group in insoluble difficulties. It would be almost impossible to avoid discussion about the doctrinal and theological principles on which the matter depends (about the rights of the Church in civil matters, etc.) and once such a discussion started (a discussion which is particularly difficult and slippery) the positive work which the group could do would evaporate.

I am convinced that the essential thing is to go ahead with creative work. The essential task is to make appreciation and love for the works of the mind penetrate more deeply into the Catholic community, and to educate it by the same token to understand better the multiplicity of views in cultural matters of Catholics equally attached to the truths involved in their faith. This can be done in walking, in going ahead, better than in discussing incidental issues and entering into conflict with the hierarchy.

Assuming that your group adopted the first conception I have mentioned, it would have time to acquire moral authority and make clear to everybody its own intellectual and religious positions. As long as these conditions are not realized, any incidental manifestations would lead only to the worst misunderstandings.

No doubt, if the group publishes a periodical, such and such a piece by a contributor will occasion more or less sharp attacks from other Catholics, perhaps from some official circles. Then he will have to defend himself, and his own thought and creative activity, as strongly as is just.

This is entirely different from taking as a group the initiative of "attack" in connection with some event or other in which certain members of the hierarchy are already involved.

The result, in such a case, would be, I am afraid, that the moral authority you might acquire among Catholics would be jeopardized from the start, for you would not be in a position to make the soundness of your view recognized (supposing that you would not be carried along to take yourselves questionable positions or to make theological missteps).

All these considerations, which have a very general bearing, explain why in my opinion it would be a big mistake to begin with the collective manifestation projected about the *Miracle*. Allen spoke his mind on the matter in the clearest manner. Now I do not think that either he or your group should become crusaders or martyrs for this picture, and set your collective activity off on a sidetrack, with no outlet.

I am sorry that this letter will perhaps disappoint you. I am more and more convinced that personal constructive work alone matters, keeping aloof from incidental issues as long as it does not become inevitable, and that the essential task with which Catholic writers and their friends in other professions are confronted is to foster and promote this constructive work.

With every kind personal regard,

Cordially yours,
Jacques Maritain

ALLEN TATE TO ROBERT FITZGERALD

1801 University Avenue, S. E.
Minneapolis 14, Minnesota
March 1, 1952

Dear Robert:

After I sent you the telegram [requesting that action in the case of *The Miracle* be at least postponed] on Wednesday I became involved in university matters; there was no time until this morning to write you the considered explanation of my request that I was oligated to give you as soon as possible.[1] What I want to bring up for further thought by the Committee of Catholics for Cultural Action is the present position of the group in the wider context of the church. I want to emphasize the distinct probability that, with all good will, we are about to act outside that context. Should this be true, we shall fail in our ultimate purposes. These purposes, I am now convinced, in view of the imminent danger, should be reexamined.

Father Lynch arrived in Minneapolis, at my invitation, on Wednesday morning, to discuss with me the question of my public relation to the Church. I had invited him to come four months ago when my removal to this city had given me a certain perspective on my problems as a Catholic writer. I was much pleased that Father Lynch thought the matter important enough to make the long trip at a time when I could not go to see him. But this problem pertains to my particular case. The larger problem of the relation of the Committee to the Church naturally developed in the course of our conversations. The views that I am about to express are partly the result of these talks with Father Lynch, and partly the result of talks last year with Jacques Maritain and Frank Sheed.[2]

I should like to put before you four points for the immediate consideration of the group:

1. In the coming generation of the Church the layman will have perhaps unprecedented influence. Under the spiritual authority of the

Church, we shall, if we are equal to the task, participate in the new cultural leadership. All signs point to this.

2. It would be a serious mistake in the politics of a new Catholic humanism to involve our group in the ambiguities of an immediate crisis, such as that created by the case of *The Miracle*. Before we can act intelligibly in specific social and political issues we must not only publicize the general articles of a Catholic humanism; we must allow enough time for our reasoned position to be considered and assimilated by the Church.

3. Precipitate action, such as filing a Brief with the New York Supreme Court, will inevitably place us with other persons and groups, Catholic, Protestant, and non-religious, who are clearly opposing the Church. At the present moment an ill-advised and irresponsible book by Thomas Sugrue is appearing: the crude methods of the press will inevitably associate us with this kind of "Catholic" anti-Catholicism.[3] The Church itself will so see us, because we have not had time to convince the Church of the integrity of our motives and of the firm Catholicism of our intellectual position.

4. It would therefore be unfortunate if *any* action were taken before we have created the larger context in which specific opinions and actions would appear in just perspective and scale.

The four points are phrased too abstractly, but I hope that they will suggest to the group certain definite applications. My own specific proposals for consideration and possible adoption by the group are as follows:

1. That a group be formed under a name that will clearly indicate a tradition of Catholic humanism.

2. That this association draw up, after due deliberation, a far-reaching philosophy for a Catholic humanism.

3. That this philosophy be set forth in a pamphlet and widely circulated.

4. That the association feel no commitment to take action in public affairs, its position in this matter to be governed by the eventual implications of its philosophy as this will be determined by Proposal 2.

Our program should thus be cultural enrichment from *within* the Church. A too self-conscious desire to convince the general public that we are enlightened Catholics should be no part of our fundamental purpose, though the existence of such an association may well redound incidentally to the credit of the Church. Our aim should be the advancement of humanistic culture within the Church herself for the greater glory of God. For the glory of God will be advanced by the deepest culture of the social order of which the Members of the Mystical Body are capable. As such a program develops, its influence would inevitably extend beyond the Catholic community. But this extrinsic result cannot be achieved as a conscious aim. A great Catholic culture as an end in itself—that should be, as I see it, the aim, simple and ambitious, of an association of Catholic men of letters. The chief end must be pursued through the practice of the arts of letters, not through propaganda.

I am sure that I do not need to remind you that the views expressed here are substantially the same as those I explained to you and others last year. I have never favored the existence of a group for political action, such as the sensational French group which formerly published *L'Action Française*.[4] The internal purpose of our association should be the comfort and inspiration of a common ideal in letters; the external purpose, the supervision and the propagation of literary standards: in the end a single purpose that shall be guided by the counsel of the Holy Ghost.

Ever affectionately yours in Christ,
Allen Tate

1. The bracketed phrase is Tate's handwritten footnote to the typescript of the letter.
2. Francis Joseph Sheed (1897–1981) was an Australian-born Roman Catholic lay theologian, lecturer, author, and publisher. He was father of the American novelist Wilfred Sheed.
3. Thomas Sugrue, *A Catholic Speaks His Mind on America's Religious Conflict* (New York, 1952).
4. A royalist, anti-Semitic, nationalistic group led by Charles Maurras. It was condemned by Pope Pius XI in 1926.

JACQUES MARITAIN TO MGR. R. FONTENELLE

Hôtel St. James
211 rue Saint-Honoré
Paris
24 August 1952

Dear Monseigneur and friend,

Permit me to recommend heartily for your warmest reception my very dear friend Allen Tate. He is not only our friend, but also our godson,—he was converted two years ago (his wife, who is also a well-known writer in the United States, had preceded him by several years).

Allen is one of the best poets and critics in the United States. He has accomplished over the past twenty years a significant oeuvre in his country, by opposing positivistic trends and by renewing, with his friends in the *New Criticism*, the whole orientation of American criticism. The humanists' teaching in American universities has deeply felt his influence, and he has an exceptional authority in literary circles. His conversion to Catholicism has in this regard a particular significance, and I believe he is destined to serve as guide to many among the intellectual youth of America.

So I would fervently wish that the Holy Father would see fit to accord him a private audience, as an eminent representative of contemporary American literature.

I also fervently wish that Mgr. Montini would kindly grant him an audience. He will surely be interested in all the first-hand information that Allen can give him on intellectual movements in America, and the recent phenomenon of Catholicism's new inroads into the American artistic and literary world.

Raïssa sends you all her thanks for your dear and generous letter, which touched both of us infinitely. Nervous exhaustion due to overwork kept me from going this year to Rome as I had planned. I'm putting off that hope until next summer. What a joy it will be to see you again.

Pray for us, dear Monseigneur and friend.

> Very respectfully yours,
> Jacques Maritain

CORNELIA BORGERHOFF TO ALLEN TATE
AND CAROLINE GORDON

> 26 Linden Lane
> Princeton, New Jersey
> March 31st, 1954

Mr. and Mrs. Allen Tate
Villa Aurelia
Porta san Pancrazio
Rome

Dear Mr. and Mrs. Tate:

Jacques and Raïssa Maritain have asked me to write to you on their behalf to inform you that Jacques had a slight heart attack last Friday. It was caused by a broken blood vessel, and the wound has already begun to heal. The doctor is entirely satisfied with his condition now, but has of course prescribed absolute rest for a number of weeks.

Vera joins Jacques and Raïssa in sending warmest thanks for your last letter, and love to you both and to Don Giovanni.[1]

Sincerely,
Cornelia N. Borgerhoff

1. Father Giovanni de Menasce, mentioned in No. 34.

CORNELIA BORGERHOFF TO ALLEN TATE

190 Prospect Avenue
Princeton, N.J.
October 9, 1960

Professor Allen Tate
University of Minnesota
Minneapolis 14, Minnesota

Dear Mr. Tate:

Jacques Maritain has asked me to write to you to give you news of him and of Raïssa. They left for France late last June, intending to return to Princeton in October. But almost immediately after their arrival in Paris Raïssa suffered a stroke. She made a good initial recovery, and Jacques was very hopeful until last month, when her condition took a turn for the worse. I fear that her strength is gradually declining.

Their address is 36 rue de Varenne, Paris 7.

I deeply regret being obliged to give you this news.

Sincerely,
Cornelia Borgerhoff

CORNELIA BORGERHOFF TO ALLEN TATE

190 Prospect Avenue
Princeton, N.J.
October 24, 1960

Dear Mr. Tate:

Thank you for your letter. My most recent news from Jacques (a letter dated Oct. 18th) indicates that Raïssa's condition is more or less the same as it has been for many weeks, but she is gradually losing strength. She can eat almost nothing, and is being sustained by daily intravenous feedings. She is lucid, but very weak. The doctors do not give Jacques any hope for her recovery, but say that the present situation may last for some time. As for Jacques himself, I need not say what anguish he is suffering. However, he continues to work; he is correcting proofs of his big new book, *Traité de la Morale*.[1] It is to be published soon in France. Later a translation will appear in this country.

I was terribly distressed to realize from your letter that you did not know of Vera's death, here in Princeton, last December. She had been bedridden for a year.

> Sincerely yours,
> Cornelia Borgerhoff

1. Jacques Maritain, *La philosophie morale: Examen historique et critique des grands systêmes* (Paris, 1960), published in America as *Moral Philosophy: An Historical and Critical Survey of the Great Systems* (New York, 1964).

SISTER MARIE PASCALE TO CAROLINE GORDON

> Toulouse, 18 March 1968

Dear Mrs. Tate:

Jacques has asked me to write to you for him; he has just received your letter, which touched him a great deal. He would have wished to do it himself, but his doctor has prescribed absolute rest. So I ask you to excuse him until he can take up the pen again, and I send you his faithful remembrance as well as his most affectionate thoughts.

> Yours very sincerely,
> Sister Marie Pascale

NOTES FROM AN INTERVIEW WITH FRANCIS FERGUSSON

Fergusson began by commenting on Jacques Maritain's influence on English-speaking poets. He said that T. S. Eliot spoke French well enough to understand Maritain and that there was no noticeable language barrier between the two, only a difference in philosophies. R. P. Blackmur knew very little French. Allen Tate was somewhat weak in French, but Tate and Maritain seemed to communicate well in English.

When asked when Tate began reading Thomas Aquinas, Fergusson replied that it was Maritain who motivated Tate to read Aquinas. According to Fergusson, Maritain was a major influence on Tate's Thomism and on his conversion to Catholicism.

Fergusson commented that he thought some of Tate's best poetry was written after he became friends with Maritain—"The Seasons of the Soul," especially.[1] Maritain was not only a personal and spiritual influence but a literary inspiration. Tate "was caught in that modern mess of skepticism plus knowledge. And he wrote some pretty difficult poems for quite a while. But 'The Seasons of the Soul,' I think, are fairly clear."

Fergusson's own work on Dante, he said, predated Maritain's chapter on Dante in *Creative Intuition in Art and Poetry*. He doubted that Maritain had influenced him in that respect.[2] Maritain did lead Fergusson to French Thomist writers and to Thomism and confirmed his interest in Aristotle. "I'm beginning to see how useful his philosophy was for finding one's way around in the modern world. It helps in all sorts of contexts. It enabled Tate to write his essay about Poe, for example, that whole line which he began as a result of Maritain. And that kept him going for quite a while."[3]

Fergusson observed that Maritain was good at articulating truths dimly perceived by everyone. "If you get messed up in modern philoso-

1. Written in 1943, "The Seasons of the Soul" appears in Allen Tate, *Poems, 1922–1947* (New York, 1948), 27–39.

2. In fact, we learn from the letters (Nos. 24 and 29, *e.g.*) that Maritain's chapter on Dante was a result of Fergusson's and Tate's influence on him.

3. See note 2 of No. 23 herein.

phy enough, it's very much of a release to have some of these ancient truths pointed out. And that does constitute an influence." Maritain's *The Degrees of Knowledge* "hit me very hard when I first read it, and I think that is the clue to his whole philosophy and point of view. He doesn't say very much directly about art in that book if I remember, but he outlines the whole human situation, and so forth, and that's what I needed at that point. . . . It's an Aristotelian approach to epistemology . . . very important."[4]

Tate, Fergusson remarked, "had a very heavy dose of Maritain for several years." He "was hardly converted for a year before he began going to the Pope and suggesting that the Pope do things to change the Catholic line. Tate doesn't have a very good sense of perspective as far as his role in the world goes. And he's been excommunicated. . . . Now he goes to mass but can't take communion and so forth." Tate was never orthodox, Fergusson stated, in spite of his Thomism. He admired the Church but objected to many contemporary Catholic policies. He was much less interested in politics than Maritain. And he fit into the twentieth century much less well than Maritain. "I think he's an excellent poet, especially in . . . 'Seasons of the Soul,' but he does *not* fit into the contemporary scene, so far as I can make out."

Raïssa Maritain's poetry was "too personal, self-indulgent. Tate also took a dim view of it."

Maritain did not come across as an aggressive proselytizer for his faith, Fergusson said. "He knew that I was not a Catholic, of course, and he seemed to accept that without blame or dismay of any kind. Maybe he thought I was headed that way, but he never suggested it in what he said." In the 1950s, Maritain appeared not to have backed off from his mission as a winner of souls in the artistic community. "When he was writing *Creative Intuition*, he was still thinking of himself as ambassador to artistic types, I think."

4. Jacques Maritain, *Distinguish to Unite; or, The Degrees of Knowledge*, trans. Gerald Phelan (New York, 1959).

INDEX